The Wigtownshire Companion

For Callum, Fergus and Jamie Crosbie.

THE WIGTOWNSHIRE COMPANION

Haig Gordon

Galloway Publishing
Kirkcudbright

Published in Scotland
by
Galloway Publishing
an imprint of
Glen Murray Publishing
The Studio, Gas Lane
Kirkcudbright
Kirkcudbrightshire
DG6 4HX
www.gallowaypublishing.co.uk

ISBN
Paper-bound
9780955318344

A CIP catalogue record for this book
is available from the British Library.

Printed in Scotland
by Bell and Bain, Glasgow

Contents

Acknowledgements

As with *The Kirkcudbrightshire Companion*, I am immeasurably indebted to Norman Chalmers for a host of lovely photographs. Here's how dedicated he was to illustrating the book: after a complete set of pictures disappeared in a theft of his equipment, he returned to the Shire and shot them all over again. The man is a hero.

The use of *Lady Agnew of Lochnaw* is courtesy of the National Galleries of Scotland, and *Loreley* is courtesy of the Tate Galleries.

Other images have been kindly supplied by David R Collin, Andrew McNeillie, Glen Murray, Alastair Reid, Historic Scotland, The Cinema Newton Stewart/J&B Print, Logan Botanic Garden, Stair Estates, Whithorn Photographic Group and The Whithorn Trust and Geograph photographers David Baird, Archie Cochrane, Colin Kinnear, Colin MacDonald, Ally McGurk, David Metcalf, Slidzenicely and Jeff Wells.

Thanks to Mr and Mrs Knott for allowing Norman to photograph Glenwhan Garden.

For the use of quotations I am grateful to the following authors or their estates: the estate of James Barke *Land of the Leal* (Canongate); Donna Brewster *The House that Sugar Built* (G C Books); Billy Kay *The Scottish World* (Mainstream); Donald MacIntosh *Travels in Galloway* (Neil Wilson Publishing); Andrew McNeillie *Ian Niall: Part of his Life* (Clutag Press); the estate of Gavin Maxwell *The House of Elrig* (Birlinn) and *Raven Seek Thy Brother* (Penguin); the estate of H V Morton *In Scotland Again* (Methuen); the estate of Edwin Muir *Scottish Journey* (Mainstream); the estate of Ian Niall (John McNeillie) *Wigtown Ploughman* (G C Books) and *A Galloway Childhood* (Heinemann); Alastair Reid *Oases* (Canongate) and *Inside Out* (Polygon); Aline Templeton *Cold in the Earth* (Hodder).

My thanks to Rena Peebles for dealing so good-humouredly with my inquiries about Drummore.

If you knew the extent to which publisher Glen Murray has kept me right, you would expect to see his credit as co-author. Another hero!

Introduction

As far as I can tell, the last book about Wigtownshire in general was published exactly a century ago. That was Sir Andrew Agnew's *Wigtownshire – A Guide for Visitors* (1908). Delightful though that work by such a distinguished member of the local gentry may be, it is probably fair to say that the time for another is long overdue.

Not that there is any shortage of excellent books relating to the area. Innes Macleod's *Discovering Galloway*, his and Ian L Donnachie's *Old Galloway* and Andrew McCulloch's *Galloway: A Land Apart*, all published since the 1970s, are outstanding works of modern scholarship. But, as their titles make clear, their frame of reference is the larger region of which Wigtownshire is but one half.

The other (eastern) half of Galloway is of course Kirkcudbrightshire, as a native of which I experienced from early boyhood onwards a strong sense of the difference between the two counties, if only because of the obvious impact on the character of Wigtownshire of its long and close relationship with its cross-channel neighbour Ireland (the subject of a separate chapter in Part 2). To put it another way: as a frequent visitor during my formative years I could hardly believe that, with no great distances involved, the people of an adjacent county could speak in such a very different way from what I was used to in my own wee part of Galloway.

In recent times, sadly, the distinction between these two venerable counties has become somewhat blurred by the insensitive reorganisation of local government. In the 1970s, when a new greater region of Dumfries and Galloway was created, one of its lower-tier administrative units, 'Wigtown District', was allowed to encroach well into the customary territory of Kirkcudbrightshire. The legacy of this has been a terrible muddling of traditional identities.

The Wigtownshire Companion, in common with its sibling *The Kirkcudbrightshire Companion*, faithfully adheres to the long-accepted vertical dividing-line of the River Cree. This precept, I am pleased to say, has the authority of an ancient pedigree. Just consider the derivation of the word Cree. It comes from *crioch* in Gaelic, the language of south-west Scotland more than one thousand years ago, and its meaning is none other than 'boundary'!

It was not just the time-honoured significance of the Cree at its eastern frontier that meant that, when the original pattern of Scotland's county councils was established in 1889, Wigtownshire

County Council was one of the most straightforward to set up. There were no ambiguities either about its other boundaries: geography dictated that. To the west and to the south the sea defines it indisputably; while to the north the Braes of Glenapp (above Cairnryan) and the high moors spreading eastwards from there create a formidably natural frontier with Ayrshire.

The county falls conveniently into three areas. The **Moors** in the north are self-explanatory. The big peninsula between Luce Bay and Wigtown Bay is known as the **Machars**, from Gaelic *machair*, 'low-lying coastal plain'. Along the west coast from the mouth of Loch Ryan down to the Mull of Galloway is the distinctively shaped **Rhins**, from Gaelic *rinn*, 'promontory'. The word is plural since this stretch of land effectively consists of two promontories back-to-back. Some folk spell it with a double-n. The validity of both spellings is reflected in the text.

As far as names are concerned, the county is fortunate in having a shorter everyday version that is widely accepted and has none of the mocking undertone of a nickname. It is, quite simply, the 'Shire'. You might think that Kirkcudbrightshire would resent its neighbour appropriating the term for itself. But there is no question of sibling rivalry over the matter. Kirkcudbrightshire has its very own pet name, the 'Stewartry', originating from medieval times when the area was administered on behalf of the Crown by a 'steward'.

The people who live in the cities of central Scotland are sometimes so parochial that they tend patronisingly to look upon the Shire as remote, perhaps even as a bit of a dead end. Well, if having Scotland's land's end makes it a dead end, then let us rejoice in that particular cul-de-sac. Land's end is equally land's beginning. In the days when power and influence came to those who ruled the waves, it wasn't much good being land-locked. Once upon a time the Shire seemed more like an international hub, at the centre of a great sea-faring crossroads of cultures and credoes. It can be of no surprise therefore that Christianity first arrived in Scotland via the shores of Luce Bay. The opening chapter of Part 2 will, I trust, put all of this into perspective and help to demonstrate how upfront this back-of-beyond was in the early phases of Scotland's evolution.

*

A final note on the arrangement of the text: it is not intended as a conventional guide-book leading you by the nose from one thing to another, and it assumes that you have bothered to equip yourself with a map. It is designed rather as a handy and easy-to-use repository of all that anyone except a specialist would need to know for a reasonably good understanding of how the Shire became what it is. Wherever you happen to be in the county, you should be able to find out more about it by looking up the nearest town or village in Part 1 - The Places. Each place description has cross-references to relevant sections of Part 2 - Themes and Personalities.

Enjoy! I did.

Part One

THE PLACES

Ardwell - Wigtown

Ardwell

An estate village associated with **Ardwell House**. The house itself is an example of what architectural historians call 'recovered'. The original building of about 1720 was smothered by additions in the 1870s. In the 1950s these attachments were stripped away.

The village is uplifted by its bonnie **kirk**. The nearest place of worship had previously been at Stoneykirk well to the north of the village. So Sir Mark and Lady McTaggart Stewart (a McTaggart of Southwick in Kirkcudbrightshire married the Stewart heiress in 1866) decided to have one built for Ardwell. They commissioned the Glasgow architect Peter MacGregor Chalmers (1859-1922), who was the leading ecclesiastical specialist in Scotland at the time as well as an acknowledged expert on medieval architecture.

The kirk was built between 1900 and 1902. Chalmers regarded his design as 'my best work as yet'. Before the building started, however, the Stewarts became concerned by an overrun on the cost estimates and suggested saving money by compromising on the quality of materials. The architect proposed instead that the building of the belfry could be left until a later date:

Ardwell kirk

> I am always loathe to suggest the use of inferior materials in a church. I am very confident from former and frequent experience that a work that is well carried out in good material and with good workmanship has a far finer look to the cultured eye, even although the work is incomplete, than another work complete in all its parts, yet cheaply and poorly executed – and there is something nice in leaving work for other days and other hands.

Clearly, the architect got his way – and did not have to sacrifice the belfry either.

Ardwell House and gardens

The **gardens** of Ardwell House are known for their displays of azaleas, cammelias and rhododendrons; and are open to the public. The grounds contain a medieval **motte** on which a castle once stood.

To the south-west a pile of stones is all that remains of **Killasser Castle**, a fifteenth- or sixteenth-century stronghold of the McCullochs. The name may be an ecclesiastical reference: the *cill* (Gaelic, 'church') of Lassair, a seventh-century Irish abbess.

Due west, Ardwell Point is the seaside site of a **broch**, a building type unique to Scotland but more usually found in Shetland, Orkney, Caithness, the Western Isles and along the coast of the north-west mainland. A circular shape and the use of unmortared

'Doon Castle' broch

stone are the principal features they all have in common. The outer wall was matched by an inner, and the space in-between, as well as having the staircase, was adapted into small rooms. The characteristic convex-concave profile of the outer wall was not unlike a modern cooling-tower. This one, frequently but misleadingly referred to as 'Doon Castle', is probably from the first century AD. Its presence here, so far from true broch-land, is a bit of a mystery. Archaeologists now do not believe that it indicates a migration of people from the north. The current theory is that there were itinerant specialist broch-builders and that a local chieftain, wary of the Roman infiltration of the Solway area, may have commissioned it. Essentially, however, the Ardwell broch remains a puzzle. Wigtownshire has another broch site near Stairhaven.

Further to the south-east are the remains of the Logan **windmill**, built towards the end of the seventeenth century. There is a contemporary description of its usefulness: 'The countrey hereabouts especially in the summer time is very defective of mills, by reason that the little bourns [burns] are then dried up; to supply which defect the Laird of Logan hath lately built an excellent windmill, which is very useful not only to his own hands but to the whole countrey thereabouts.' In the early nineteenth century it was converted into a meal mill.

Auchness - a 17th-century tower house with 19th-century additions which is still inhabited

To the south of Ardwell, **Auchness** is a tower-house of about 1600. Most of the other bits are nineteenth-century.

Bladnoch

Now absorbed into Wigtown but proudly retaining an identity of its own at the foot of the hill, alongside the **river** from which it takes its name. The village grew up around the river crossing-point on the route taking medieval pilgrims to the shrine of Ninian at Whithorn. The present **bridge** was constructed in the 1860s, replacing one of 1710. There was also a railway bridge a short distance downstream. This was the biggest single civil engineering component along the Wigtownshire line from Newton Stewart south to Whithorn, stage two in the development of the county's railways. The bridge was demolished following the line's closure in 1950. Bladnoch did not have its own station but it did have a siding, which was useful for the local **creamery**, a building of 1899 which is now incorporated into an industrial estate.

Bladnoch Distillery is one of the few Lowland malt whisky distilleries, and certainly the southernmost. It has undergone a remarkable re-birth. Opened in 1817, it was closed down in 1993. However, the following year the plant was acquired by Raymond Armstrong, a businessman from across the water in County Down. At first he envisaged it as a holiday home but then decided to revive the distilling. 'I didn't want to run out of Bladnoch!'

Operations re-started in 2000. As of old, the water supply is brought to the distillery via a special cut from one and a half miles upstream, since the River Bladnoch is still tidal where it passes the plant itself. The whisky has been described by a professional connoisseur as having 'a light, fragrant, lemony aroma and a gentle, unassertive flavour with fruity tones'.

The well defended ruins of Baldoon Castle

South of the village, only a fragment of the sixteenth/seventeenth-century **Baldoon Castle** remains, but one or two legends live on. In particular, Baldoon is reputed to have provided Sir Walter Scott with material for his novel *The Bride of Lammermoor* (1819). The cross-over between fact and fiction makes for much confusion.

First the 'facts' of the novel. Lucy, daughter of Sir William and Lady Ashton, falls in love with the Master of Ravenswood. Because the prospective groom is not rich enough, her parents oppose their marriage and Lucy is forced into wedlock with a man of their choice, the Laird of Bucklaw. Ravenswood arrives on the scene after the ceremony has taken place, challenging the husband to a duel. But it is Lucy who kills her new spouse by stabbing him. She too dies, shortly after going insane.

Now the bald facts of Baldoon. Janet, eldest daughter of the 1st Viscount Stair (see Part 2 - Celebrities of the Shire), wished to marry Lord Rutherford. Her parents preferred as a future son-in-law the considerably wealthier David, heir to Sir David Dunbar of Baldoon. In 1669, under intense parental pressure, Janet submitted to this marriage plan but nineteen days after the nuptials she mysteriously died.

These facts then appear to have been embellished, possibly maliciously by Viscount Stair's enemies, into various versions of a legend. One has Janet killing her husband; another has the husband killing Janet; a third has the jilted suitor as the husband's assassin. The kernel of the legend is of course rather more excit-

An artist's impression of the Baldoon nuptials

ing than the real-life account, and it was that which gave Scott part of his story, which is set in East Lothian, a long way from Baldoon Castle.

Janet Dalrymple is said to reappear from time to time as the 'White Lady of Baldoon'! Her presence was apparently not felt in the autumn of 2007 when Scottish Opera gave an open-air performance of Gaetano Donizetti's *Lucia di Lammermoor* (1835), which was based on Scott's novel. The local newspaper reported: 'In contrast to the dark deeds of that day which presaged Janet's miserable death exactly one month later, a glorious autumn sun set behind the stage during an enchanting evening of story and song.'

During the Second World War Baldoon was the location for **RAF Wigtown** (see Part 2 - Wartime Wigtownshire).

The derelict control tower of RAF Wigtown now stands forlornly among bales of hay on what used to be the runway - Wigtown is in the background on the right

Cairnryan

A significant **port** since the 1700s when the cattle trade brought brisk business, and now, after some downs as well as ups, born again as a terminal for some of the cross-channel Irish ferries.

During the **Second World War** Cairnryan was elevated to strategic importance and a massive re-construction programme was undertaken to transform it into an emergency back-up in the event of Clydeside being destroyed by German bombing. It had a dedicated transport link, the Cairnryan Military Railway (see Part 2 - Wartime Wigtownshire).

The military pier and lighthouse at Cairnryan

Cairnryan Military Port never was required for use in that role and in February 1944 it was placed on a 'care and maintenance' basis. It was only in peacetime that the harbour found renewed purpose, becoming a leading centre for the disposal of surplus military hardware. Soon after hostilities ceased in 1945, eighty-six U-boats surrendered by the Germans were brought to Loch Ryan. The sight of this armada of vessels, which until so recently had posed such a threat, caused much excitement locally, especially when, over a weekend, one of them was opened to the public and five thousand people visited.

The U-boats were in Loch Ryan, however, not for public entertainment but for scuttling in the Irish Sea. Thirty-six of them never made it to the scuttling point some 180 miles from Loch Ryan. They were in such a poor condition that on the way to the deep-sea scrapyard they just sank of their own accord.

Concrete 'pontoon boats' north of Cairnryan
- a reminder of the village's wartime role

Cairnryan at this time was also involved in the dumping at sea of surplus explosives. This was hazardous work, and on one occasion seven workers were killed and fifteen seriously injured when the explosives they were handling went off. The chosen dump site was Beaufort's Dyke, a long, narrow trough at the bottom of the North Channel between Wigtownshire and Northern Ireland. According to the Ministry of Defence, Cairnryan was ideal as a base for this operation: 'It was particularly suitable because not only could ocean-going shipping – required for dumpings and vessel scuttlings in very deep water in the Atlantic – use deep-water berths away from commercial traffic, but it was also sited quite close to the Beaufort's Dyke Explosives Dumping Ground.'

The discarded material included chemical weapons. Fifty years later fears were raised about possible environmental damage from these disposals. The government's Marine Laboratory in Aberdeen undertook a survey and found that there was 'no pollution of the marine environment by conventional or chemical munitions'. Not everyone found this statement reassuring.

In 1997 Beaufort's Dyke was again causing controversy. It was discovered that radioactive material had also been deposited there during the 1950s. The material, encased in concrete within steel drums, consisted largely of laboratory waste from Glasgow and Edinburgh universities. The government attempted to allay public disquiet by stating that 'the amounts of radioactivity that they contain are so small that release of their contents would be of no significance in terms of either public health or the marine environment.'

Intermittently for some thirty years after the war, Cairnryan was used for the breaking-up of ships. From 1948 redundant battleships were dismantled here, as were the aircraft carriers *HMS Eagle* (in 1978) and *HMS Ark Royal* (in 1980).

Cairnryan's status as a military port officially came to an end in 1959. Cairnryan Military Railway was removed in 1967.

To the north of the harbour, at Cairn Point, Loch Ryan **lighthouse** was built in 1847 under the supervision of Alan Stevenson, uncle of the writer Robert Louis Stevenson.

East of the lighthouse, **Lochryan House** was begun in 1701 for a branch of the Agnew family. Its striking battlemented features, according to an architectural historian, 'can be regarded either as a last assertion of the tower-house or as an anticipation of romanticism'. Calling in en route for Portpatrick in 1769, the Ayrshire-born man of letters James Boswell was much taken by this 'neat house': 'I had a great desire to buy this place. It was such a one as I had often fancied in a romantic mood, and I thought I and my companion could live at it most happily.' For Boswell the bright lights of London beckoned instead.

Castle Kennedy

A nineteenth-century village created to house the estate workers of the Earls of Stair, taking its name from the ancient fortification within the laird's parkland.

The history of the land now known and marketed as Castle Kennedy Gardens is rich and complex. There are two castles, an old kirk and an Iron Age crannog site, all within a striking setting of two lochs, the White and the Black, divided by an isthmus. When the traveller and writer George Borrow passed by here in 1866 he noted in his diary: 'the most beautiful scenery I ever saw' (whether he meant the most beautiful he ever saw *anywhere* or just in Wigtownshire, is not clear).

There was castle here from the 1400s, but what can be seen now within the earl's grounds are the remains of the **Castle Kennedy** built around 1600 for John Kennedy, 5th Earl of Cassilis. The castle and grounds were sold in 1674 to Sir James Dalrymple, later 1st Viscount Stair (see Part 2 - Celebrities of the Shire). In 1716 the castle was destroyed by fire and never again lived in. The Stairs, by then with an earldom, established a new seat at Culhorn to the west.

With the ruins of Castle Kennedy as a picturesque focal-point, the Stairs began from 1730 the creation of **formal gardens** along the isthmus. At the south-east end a canal was made to link the

Castle Kennedy

lochs on either side. Work on fashioning the gardens continued until 1747, after which they were neglected for a century. In 1840 the 8th Earl of Stair, having found the original designs, set about restoring and extending the gardens, employing the London-based Scottish landscape architect J C Loudon. Estate cottages were removed and this was when the workers were re-located to the new village of Castle Kennedy. At the same time they also got a new place of worship, **Inch Parish Kirk**, a good chunk of which is taken up by the exclusive Stair Pew. This building replaced **Inch Old Parish Kirk**, now roofless, which is on the west side of the White Loch and was built in 1770, though the site had been ecclesiastical long before that.

In the seventeenth century the Earl of Cassilis used to cross from old Castle Kennedy to the kirk by boat, thus avoiding the longer round journey by land. The nearby tiny island in White Loch had a house which the Earl would inhabit on the Sabbath; there he 'us'd to retire himselfe betwixt sermons'!

When re-establishing the garden project the 8th earl may have had in mind the building of a new house in the grounds, but it was not until 1864 that the 10th Earl began what is now **Lochinch Castle**, at the other end of the isthmus from the ruins of Castle Kennedy. The chosen style was the then fashionable Scots Baronial but with French trimmings, the latter a tribute no doubt to the Countess, Louisa, daughter of the Duc de Coigny. It is of course not a 'castle' at all but an example of the revivalist castellated chic that was so dear to the hearts of Victorian Scotland.

Lochinch Castle

The **isthmus** on which both the old and the new castles sit was once an island within a single stretch of water then known as Loch Inch (from Gaelic *innis*, 'island'). There was a local belief, when the loch was divided not by an isthmus but by an island, that the distinction between the 'white' and 'black' sections was reflected within the fish population:

> ...there are two several sorts of trout; the one blacker than the other, and each keep their own part of the loch; so that, when they are in the dish at the table, those that are acquainted with the differences can easily tell in which part of the loch such and such a fish was taken.
>
> [Andrew Symson]

To the east of the village, **Castle Kennedy Airfield** originally came into use in 1913 when Galloway's first recorded landing of a fixed-wing craft took place in August of that year. There were six of them, all from the Royal Flying Corps squadron based near Montrose on the north-east coast; they were en route for Ireland. During the Castle Kennedy stopover they were fitted with flotation bags in case they had to ditch into the Irish Sea. Three of the aircraft developed technical problems and were not able to join the others on the return flight to Montrose. Their appearance at the airfield here caused such excitement that schools were closed for the day and special trains arrived at Castle Kennedy station packed with eager eye-witnesses.

During the Second World War the airfield became one of the plethora of military bases throughout the county (see Part 2 - Wartime Wigtownshire). This one had an air gunnery school. The airfield is still partially available for landings, but its flat expanse is more commonly used these days for karting. This is where the Formula One racing driver David Coulthard used to come, from his home in neighbouring Kirkcudbrightshire, to get his early experiences of speed.

To the south-west of the village, **Soulseat** is the site of Wigtownshire's missing abbey. It was developed in the twelfth century on a peninsula sticking out into Soulseat Loch and was a foundation possibly by Fergus, Lord of Galloway, for the Premonstratensian Order. Nothing is clear about its history and now not a trace of it remains, the manse for the Inch parish minister having been built on the site.

Challoch

A clachan that is not much more than just **All Saints Church**, an Episcopal chapel put up in the 1870s for Edward Stopford Blair, owner of nearby Penninghame House. His death in 1885 is marked by a marble cross in the grounds.

Penninghame House, a nineteenth-century country mansion built in a seventeenth-century style, was completed in 1869. From 1954 until 2000 it was an open prison, a last-stage establishment for inmates reaching the end of their sentences, the first of its type in Scotland. When the plans for it were announced there was some public disquiet but in time 'the fears of the townspeople were so completely removed that many of the inmates were made welcome into the communal life of the district' [*The Third Statistical Account of Scotland*]. Lags and locals came together in activities such as sport and amateur drama.

Penninghame House is now the headquarters of an organisation calling itself Oneness University UK, which claims to 'help you attain the enlightenment state or Oneness, and support you on your journey into deeper states of consciousness'. Courses are based on *Deeksha*: 'a transfer of divine energy...brought to the world by the grace of the avatars Amma and Bhagavan'. The co-founder of Penninghame 'University' combines healing with 'his work as a highly successful property developer'.

Drummore

Scotland's **most southerly village**, the closest to the country's land's end at the Mull of Galloway, and further south than a large part of north-east England. Drummore and Durham are on about the same latitude.

Being some seventeen miles down the south Rhins from Stranraer, it has often felt neglected by the county's decision-makers and overland transport has always been a bugbear. A particular cause of resentment was that it was never connected to the nineteenth-century railway system. There were one or two schemes to extend the network down the peninsula but nothing came of them. Even as late as the end of the First World War a committee appointed by the Secretary of State for Scotland to advise on rural transport recommended a light railway from Stranraer to Drummore. The words were not followed by action.

There were various road services connecting with the Stranraer-Portpatrick line. In 1907 steam buses, with a capacity for thirty passengers, started running three times a day each way. Advertisements said they would 'stop anywhere to pick up or set down passengers, except on steep hills'. The vehicles were not reliable and there were occasional confrontations with frightened horses. The steam service did not last much more than a year.

Drummore's difficulties with transport by land meant, however, that its **harbour** remained vibrant long after most other Wigtownshire ports had become almost moribund. Bringing in heavy cargoes like coal continued to make economic sense. The present north pier was built around 1845 and extended in the late 1890s.

Drummore harbour

An early-twentieth-century description testifies to the harbour's liveliness. 'The little seaport had a considerable amount of shipping, and the erection of a jetty and breastwork has added greatly to the advantages of the natural bay as a shelter for the numerous fishing boats, oyster dredgers, and small coasting vessels that frequent it.' The schooners that plied in and out of Drummore from the mid-nineteenth century until the mid-twentieth were in many cases locally built. Drummore was not always so sleepy.

The **name** derives from Gaelic *druim mor*, 'big ridge'. Drummore has the honour of getting the very first mention in John MacQueen's magisterial *Place-Names in the Rhinns of Galloway and Luce Valley* (2002). The professor's initial interest is not, however, the village itself (that comes later) but an amusing contrast between the names of two houses. One is called 'Fineview'. The other is a waggish joke: 'Naeview'!

Visitors who take the short-cut known as the '**Slippy Passage**' from Stair Street down to Shore Street may notice a hand-rail that has been placed particularly low, and they might assume that its positioning was designed to be child-friendly. In fact it was put there as an aid for a local dwarf called Bob Cosh. As well as serving in a shop, Bob had an extra job during the 1950s as a barman at the Ship Inn. To get to and from the inn he had to use the passage, whose stone paving could be treacherous in wet weather. As he pulled pints Bob could appear to be of normal height – until he had to descend from the box on which he stood to reach the top of the bar.

The surrounding area abounds in the remains of buildings from long before the modern village grew up. At Low Drummore there was a **castle**, a sixteenth-century tower-house. To the south-west, close to the farm of High Drummore, there is a **motte**, the site of an earlier fortification. Further south, on the way to the Mull, are various sites associated with St Medan (see Kirkmaiden). Just to the east of Barracks Bridge and beside the Kirk Burn are the remains of the **original kirk of Kirkmaiden**. Some worshippers must have reached the kirk by water, for the adjacent shore by Luce Bay is called **Portankill**, meaning 'harbour of the church' from the Gaelic *port na cille*. Down the coast from Portankill is a religious hideaway known as **St Medan's Cave**, a natural rock formation enhanced by built stonework. Close by are the **Chapel Wells**, once a kind of local health spa, which, according to an account in the 1790s, 'was considered an infallible cure for almost any disease...till no very remote period, it was customary for almost the whole population of the parish to collect at this spot on the first Sabbath of May...to bathe in the well, to leave their gifts in the cave, and to spend the day in gossiping or amusements'.

Due south is the **Mull of Galloway**, Scotland's 'Land's End'. The lighthouse, designed by Robert Louis Stevenson's grandfather,

Mull of Galloway lighthouse

The spectacular location of the award-winning Gallie Craig coffee house

was completed in 1830. A fog-horn was placed at the water's edge in 1894. Supplies for the keepers used to be brought by boat and landed at the little port of East Tarbet. One of the benefits of the introduction of the lighthouse was that skippers no longer mistook Luce Bay for the Firth of Clyde; many shipwrecks along the Luce coastline can be attributed to that early misapprehension. The lighthouse was automated in 1988.

Visitors to this windswept headland can now enjoy the comforts of the **Gallie Craig** coffee house, which takes its name from the rock at the very tip of this southernmost part of Scotland. The architects for this facility were instructed to make a minimal impact on the landscape, and to this effect the roof is covered by turf, thus not spoiling the view for the gulls flying overhead (very considerate).

The cliffs around the lighthouse are home to an estimated three and a half thousand pairs of breeding **seabirds**, making this spot the largest mainland colony of its type in south-west Scotland. Since 1975 the Royal Society for the Protection of Birds has run a nature reserve here. Apart from the kittiwakes, fulmars, puffins and shags, the area is rich in butterfly life, while anyone gazing out to sea may be able to spot a grey seal, a porpoise and (occasionally) even a dolphin or a basking shark.

The RSPB reserve embraces, six miles out to sea eastwards, a couple of rocky islets known as the Big **Scaur** ['cliff'] and the Wee Scaur. The larger one has a colony of about two and a half thousand pairs of gannets. Many a sailing ship met its end on these treacherous obstacles. One can only wonder how the gannets coped with the World War 2 use of the isles for target practice. The Ordnance Survey has inexplicably opted to call them the Scares. Perhaps 'Big Scare' is meant as a warning to navigators.

The area around Drummore and the Mull of Galloway is traditionally associated with **heather ale**, a legendary potion brewed by prehistoric inhabitants of the south Rhins. According to the story, the last survivor of the brewing clan ensured that he died before his enemies could force out of him the secret of the recipe. The yarn has tickled the fancy of many subsequent writers, including Robert Louis Stevenson:

> From the bonny bells of heather
> They brewed a drink long-syne,
> Was sweeter far than honey,
> Was stronger far than wine.
> They brewed it and they drank it,
> And lay in a blessed swound
> For days and days together
> In their dwelling underground.

The legend of the recipe's irrecoverable disappearance did not deter F Marian McNeill, author of the classic *The Scots Kitchen* (1929), from having a go. Her ingredients are heather, hops, barm [yeast], syrup, ginger and water.

A brewery in Clackmannanshire now makes a heather ale, the method for which they describe as: 'Into the boiling bree of malted barley, sweet gale [bog-myrtle] and flowering heather are added, then after cooling slightly the hot ale is poured into a vat of fresh heather flowers where it infuses for an hour before being fermented.'

Dunragit

A strange name which may be explicable as Dun+Rheged: Gaelic *dun* is 'fort' and Rheged was the sixth-century Cumbrian kingdom whose sphere of influence embraced the northern Solway coast after the departure of the Romans. There is an ancient **motte** here called Round Dounan and this may well have been the site of the 'fort of Rheged'.

The known history of the Dunragit area goes back to **Neolithic** times. The northern fringes of Luce Bay are probably where the first human settlements occurred in what is now Galloway. A stunningly fruitful series of excavations by an archaeological team from Manchester University took place here between 1999 and 2002. In 1992 aerial photographs had identified circular patterns in the soil around **Droughduil** between the A75 main road and the Luce Bay dunes. There were three concentric circles, the biggest being about 300 metres in diameter. It appeared to have been some kind of henge, a ceremonial gathering-place. The subsequent digging unearthed support for the theories. The archaeologists found that the holes would have held timber poles forming the circles. They further found that the circles were in line with an earthwork known as Droughduil Motte. It had previously been assumed that this motte was of the medieval type; now it seemed to be contemporary with the timber henge from some 2,500 years BC. The leader of the excavations, Professor Julian Thomas, concluded: 'Historically, I think this is as important as Stonehenge'. The identification of Dunragit as a significant archaeological site was not entirely good news for its present-day inhabitants: it caused a further delay in implementing plans for a much needed by-pass.

Modern Dunragit used to be a busy place with a big **creamery** and its own **railway station** (see Part 2 - The Land and the Sea). This halt was more important than it might have appeared. The Challoch junction was nearby, which meant that this was where cross-Galloway passengers changed for the line going north to Ayrshire. 'One could only wonder at the thoughts of strangers from the distant when they found themselves turfed out into a winter blizzard in the middle of the night in this rather desolate outpost seemingly in the back of beyond,' writes Donald MacIntosh in his Wigtownshire reminiscences *Travels in Galloway*.

MacIntosh also tells the story of a Dunragit railway porter who slipped on an icy platform and found that the half-bottle of whisky, which was to have sustained him through a night-shift, had been smashed. His cry of 'Change here for Girvan, Ayr and Glasgow' suddenly turned into 'Change here for...Hell, damnation and buggery'.

Dunragit House

Dunragit House is substantially of the eighteenth century but incorporates elements from the previous century. In the 1680s the estate was acquired, in somewhat dubious circumstances, by Sir James Dalrymple, later 1st Viscount Stair (see Part 2 - Celebrities of the Shire). Dalrymple, it is said, took possession on behalf of a minor for whom he was guardian. The minor, on reaching his legal maturity, discovered, too late, that Dalrymple had pulled a fast one and deprived him of his inheritance.

A subsequent Dalrymple married an heiress of the Hays of Castle of Park (see Glenluce), and thus began the Dalrymple-Hay dynasty, which flowered in the person of Admiral Sir John Dalrymple Hay (1821-1912), naval officer and Member of Parliament (see Part 2 - Celebrities of the Shire).

The Luce Bay **dunes** at Genoch south of Dunragit village attracted the wry attention of Sir Andrew Noel Agnew, author of *Wigtownshire – A Guide for Visitors* (1908):

> These sandhills form a vast rabbit warren, where large numbers of rabbits are killed annually. Sometimes the rabbits have to surrender their burrows to the sheldrakes who breed in this locality, and love to lay their eggs in the safe obscurity of a rabbit hole.

The area north of Dunragit has one of Wigtownshire's exotic Gulf Stream gardens. **Glenwhan Gardens** have been created since the late 1970s on a once bleak hillside. In 1974 Tessa and Bill Knott bought, unseen, a dilapidated house and 103 acres. 'We found a herd of cattle and a flock of pigeons occupying our farmhouse, and the land a beautiful and untamed wilderness of rock, bracken and gorse. In fact the land was so wild that there was no garden at all.'

The first priorities were to re-built the house and to farm the land; initially there had been no intention of

creating a horticultural splash. Then Tessa got inspiration from a visit to the Logan Botanic Garden (see Port Logan) and twelve acres were set aside to be developed into what is now a popular visitor attraction between March and October.

Elrig

An intriguing name: it comes from Gaelic and means 'ambush' and in particular a trap in which deer met their end.

The cottages here were once occupied by **weavers**. The Old Mill Burn powered at one time a not inconsiderable complex of industrial activities, including a **tattie mill** (see Part 2 – The Land and the Sea). There was also a bone-meal mill until 1904, and another for oatmeal until 1913.

The grand **House of Elrig**, built to the north-west in the 1920s, was the childhood home of the writer Gavin Maxwell (see Part 2 - The Writers) and was later occupied by the Austrian artist Oskar Kokoschka (see Part 2 - Other Pairs of Eyes).

Traces of much earlier habitations are to be found to the north of the village. These are Iron Age island-homes known as **crannogs**. There is one in Elrig Loch, and another to its west at the now drained Rough Loch.

A short distance to the west of the House of Elrig a ten-year programme of excavation, starting in 1984, revealed for the first time **Barhobble**, a religious site of great antiquity. The findings were not only a now clearly visible 'lost' chapel of the 12th century but also traces of Christian use as far back as the eighth century. From about 1000 it appears to have been used as a burial ground, upon which around 1150 a stone chapel was built. From about 1300, during the disruption of the Anglo-Scottish Wars of Independence, it seems to have been abandoned.

Garlieston

A pleasing composition developed from the 1760s by Lord Garlies, later Earl of Galloway, whose mansion Galloway House (see below) had recently been built to the south. This was the main **port** for the Machars and a busy one at that, something it may be difficult to imagine today. The pier was built in the 1830s and expanded in the 1850s for the new steamships that ran regular services to and from Glasgow, the Isle of Man and Liverpool. As well as the harbour traffic there was shipbuilding (up to 100 tons), ropemaking and sailcloth manufacturing.

Galloway House is almost ludicrous in the scale of its grandiosity. Building began in the 1740s for the 6th Earl of Galloway after the family seat at Glasserton was destroyed by fire. The Earl was notoriously mean and stipulated that 'I must have cheapness primarily in view'. The designer was the then fashionable John Douglas but he delegated to another architect, John Baxter, who was on-site to deal with the aristocratic penny-pinching.

The house was subsequently altered and added to on at least five occasions. The last improvement for the Galloways was completed in 1909 and that must have finally finished them off financially, for in that same year the 11th Earl sold up and moved to the much more modest Cumloden at Minnigaff on the Kirkcudbrightshire side of the River Cree.

The house passed into the hands of Sir Malcolm McEarcharn, a businessman with roots in Islay who had made a fortune in Australia. He also had political ambitions but turned his back on Aus-

Galloway House

tralia when he lost his parliamentary seat. From Melbourne he came to the Machars. But he did not enjoy his new laird's life for long: a year after purchasing Galloway House he dropped dead in Cannes. His son Neil took over but he had aspirations elsewhere and sold the estate to concentrate on creating the now celebrated garden at Villa Taranto on Lake Maggiore.

From 1947 until 1976 Glasgow's education department used Galloway House as a residential school.

When the **railways** were expanded into the Machars peninsula in the 1870s (see Part 2 - The Land and the Sea), Garlieston nearly missed out. The Earl of Galloway, despite himself helping to promote the Wigtownshire Railway, did not want it infringing on his grand estate. So at first Garlieston was going to have to make do with a station at Millisle to the west of the village. But it was soon appreciated that this was a nonsense and the village got its own wee branch-line up to the harbour, though it lasted only until 1903.

The **Second World War** brought intense activity to Garlieston during 1943-44, when the main test-site for the Mulberry Harbour Project was at Rigg Bay, just south of Galloway House (see Part 2 - Wartime Wigtownshire).

Stone commemorating Garlieston's connection with the construction of sections of the Mulberry Harbours

Cruggleton Castle - what remains of it!

Cruggleton Castle, south from Garlieston, was the western stronghold of the Lords of Galloway during the twelfth and thirteenth centuries. But this naturally defensive site had attracted successive settlements from the Iron Age onwards. The earlier buildings had been constructed of timber. Re-construction in the thirteenth century was in stone, and there was a further stage of building in the fifteenth century. Once abandoned, the stonework was substantially removed for use in the building of drystane-dykes; hence the meagre remains of today.

To the west of the castle is the bonnie, lonesome setting for the twelfth-century **Cruggleton Kirk**, the most complete building of its period in the area, thanks in no small part to 1890s restoration commissioned by the 3rd Marquess of Bute around the same time as his re-construction of Old Place of Mochrum (see Mochrum).

All small places are rife with memories of what are invariably described as the **'old worthies'**. At a reunion of Wigtownshire folk in Glasgow in 1896, Alexander A Cuthbert entertained the audience with a raft of stories, later published as *Reminiscences of Garliestown* [the spelling has slightly changed since then]. The characters included one Davie Eadie, who was renowned for entertaining the local children. Cuthbert had 'seen him execute a dance in the progress of which he adroitly needled a stick backwards and forwards between his legs, and give an exhibition of what he

Cruggleton Kirk

called a Kirkcudbright laugh'. As a Kirkcudbright man, I can only wonder what kind of laugh a Garliestonian once deemed to be typical of my home town!

Doorway, Cruggleton Kirk

Glasserton

Now just a few houses, Glasserton was once dominated by a great mansion. Only the grounds of **Glasserton House** remain (revived in recent years as Woodfall Gardens). This was the original home of the Earls of Galloway. The first house was destroyed by fire in 1734. A smaller replacement was put up but it proved to be so unsatisfactory that the family just abandoned it. After that they re-located to the Garlieston area and began building Galloway House.

In 1767 the Glasserton land was inherited by Admiral Keith Stewart, a son of the 6th Earl of Galloway. He set about rebuilding on the site, a showy affair designed by Robert Adam. Stewart died in 1795. His widow soon re-married, his son was a minor and so the estate was put up for let, the particulars stating:

> The Pleasure Ground is extensive...The gardens contain some acres of ground, and are inclosed with Brick-walls, which are sixteen feet high, and well stocked with the choicest fruit trees. The Vinery, Peach and Nectarin Houses, as well as the Melon Beds, have lately been put in the most complete order, and produce great quantities of the choicest fruit.

According to the 1851 census, the estate workforce comprised: 11 house staff, 1 head groom, 6 men, 16 general labourers, 1 poultry maid, 1 head gardener and 2 apprentices.

Admiral Keith Stewart

During the Second World War Glasserton House was taken over as accommodation for personnel engaged in the Mulberry Harbour Project (see Part 2 - Wartime Wigtownshire). Hitler was defeated but so too was Glasserton House: in 1948 the problem of costly upkeep was radically solved – by total demolition.

Glasserton Kirk was built in the 1730s and expanded a century later. In surroundings so redolent of aristocratic pretension it is touching to see that a modest tenant, who died in 1773, gets the most effusive gravestone inscription in the kirkyard:

> Stop Passenger, the humbler virtues know
> Of one in life, that never made a foe.
> Honest and plain, and still as light was giv'n
> He trod with willing steps the path to heav'n.
> What tho' the Rich dispise the lowly kind,
> They not in God a partial Judge shall find.
> Beyond the grave all vain distinctions cease
> And only Saints are crown'd with endless peace.

Glasserton Kirk

Glenluce

The original settlement had a Gaelic name, Ballinclach. It became Clachan of Glenluce, then just Glenluce. It grew as, and to an extent remains, a place of refreshment for travellers across Galloway. In the days of cattle droving it was a trysting-place on the route to England (see Part 2 – The Land and the Sea).

In 1866 the writer George Borrow (of *Lavengro* and *Wild Wales* fame) stayed two nights here during his Galloway walking-tour, noting in his diary:

> July 18...Glenluce, regular old-fashioned Scottish town; very beautiful scenery, hollow and upland dells lined with woods; MacLellan's Hotel – ale; stroll about the town, old and thoroughly Scottish...
> Capital dinner – salmon, mutton, and sweets; first-rate water. Stroll behind the Inn. The glen, the little bridge, the rivulet and trees; child playing in the water; strong smell of turf smoke throughout the village; cool, delightful evening; stroll up and down. People in the street sitting or standing enjoying the cool...Return to Inn; sleep comfortably.
> July 19 – Breakfast – egg, ham, honeycomb...Go to see Abbey...The miller and his friends seated on the stone wall drinking cool water out of a basin; discourse about the war and the Pope of Rome. Many Papists in the neighbourhood, but all Irish, the natives all Protestants. Dinner – rice soup, salmon, mutton chop, pancake; stroll; Free Church minister preaching in a meadow...

Ruins of Glenluce Abbey

To the north-west of the village, **Glenluce Abbey**, which Borrow mentions, was founded in the 1190s by Roland, Lord of Galloway, as a Cistercian daughter-house of Dundrennan Abbey in Kirkcudbrightshire, which itself had been founded by his grandfather Fergus. There are few remains of the abbey church, though the outline of the nave, transepts and presbytery are clearly evident. The best preserved part is the late-fifteenth-century chapter-house with outstanding carvings and a ribbed ceiling that springs from a central pier. In the sixteenth century, as the monastic institutions fell foul of the Protestant Reformation, local landed families fought over the pickings (see Part 2 – The Early History). The abbey finally ceased to have a spiritual function in 1602.

To the south-west of Glenluce, the **Castle of Park** is a prominent and impressive sixteenth-century laird's tower-house, overlooking the Water of Luce. In the eighteenth century it acquired wings but they were removed around 1970. An inscription above the entrance states: 'This verk vas begun the first day of March 1590 by Thomas Hay of Park and Janet McDoual his spous'. It was Hay's father, also Thomas, who had earlier been granted the lands of Park. Hay senior was the lay administrator of Glenluce Abbey and this was apparently his reward for helping the infamously rapacious Kennedys to get ownership of the Abbey estate in the great post-Reformation land-grab by the magnates (see above). It has

Castle of Park

been claimed that Hay junior's new home was built with stone stripped from the Abbey, but that has been disputed.

Castle of Park is now run by the Landmark Trust.

Glenluce was once considered to harbour a spook. The **Devil of Luce** featured in *Satan's Invisible World Discovered* (1685), a compilation of 'authentic' examples of witches, devils and other spirits. Its author was George Sinclair, a professor of mathematics and experimental philosophy at Glasgow University. Glenluce's own wee devilish spirit is supposed to have inhabited the home of a weaver during the 1650s. The weaver allegedly spurned a beggar, who retaliated by placing a curse on him.

South-west of the village, where the Water of Luce enters Luce Bay, a stretch of merseland occasionally isolated by high tides is named after **St Helena**, the South Atlantic island to which Napoleon Bonaparte was exiled and where he was buried. To visitors the name is baffling, but the explanation can be found in the career of Wigtownshire laird Admiral Sir John Dalrymple Hay (see Part 2 - Celebrities of the Shire).

The railway viaduct over the River Luce which forms the basis of Glenluce's town emblem

Innermessan

The huge flat-topped mound of **Innermessan Motte** was part of a massive earth and timber castle built in the 12th century by Norman knights brought to the area by the Lords of Galloway. It became the centre of a large feudal estate. Much of its wealth probably came from the control of trade and shipping in Loch Ryan.

Innermessan Motte

The town that grew up around the castle was given burgh status and by the end of the Middle Ages was the largest settlement on Loch Ryan. In the seventeenth century, the powerful Kennedys decided to switch their allegiance to Stranraer and Innermessan sank into rapid decline. By the end of the 17th century it had become an insignificant hamlet. There is now virtually no trace of Wigtownshire's **'lost town'**: its abandoned stone buildings were all too tempting as ready-made quarries.

It is hard to appreciate that this now insubstantial place was once a major settlement, but in the sixteenth century the mapmaker Timothy Pont listed just three towns in Wigtownshire: Whithorn, Wigtown – and Innermessan.

Craigcaffie Castle

To the south-east lies **Craigcaffie Castle**, a tower-house built in the 1570s for John Neilson and his wife Margaret Strang. A panel above the main door shows two shields and their initials I.N. and M.S. The lands of Craigcaffie were originally granted to John, son of Neil, Earl of Carrick in the 14th century.

Little is known of the Neilsons except that they owned Craigcaffie for over 400 years. The property was bought in 1759 by McDouall of Logan, who sold it in 1791 to the Earl of Stair.

Isle of Whithorn

It may now look as if the place should be more accurately called Peninsula of Whithorn. But in fact the eastern strip of land that gives shelter to the harbour has been known to turn into an **island** at an exceptionally high tide. On one occasion at the height of the smuggling trade in the eighteenth century it provided the captain of a smugglers' ship with an unexpected means of escape from the government cutter that was in pursuit. When the smugglers sailed into Isle of Whithorn harbour, it seemed as if they had entered a trap. To the astonishment of the excise officers, the illicit craft darted back out into the open sea along a channel that would not normally have been adequate for such a substantial vessel. 'When the tide receded,' according to one account, 'a few curious seamen at the Isle examined the hazardous route of the lugger in leaving the harbour, and found a track made by the keel of the vessel in the shingly bottom about a hundred yards long. Several large stones had also been shifted. Carrying so much sail and having great way on, she had completely forced her passage through the unlikely channel.'

Isle of Whithorn Bay had been from late-medieval times the landing-place for sea-borne **pilgrims** heading for the shrine of St Ninian. (St Ninian's Chapel on the headland is not quite what its

Oyster smacks at Isle of Whithorn, late 19th century

name might suggest: see below). In the late fifteenth century King James IV often came to worship and it was he, in the early years of the sixteenth century, who authorised the creation of a **harbour**. The pier was extended around 1790, after which the quayside was busy with the export of agricultural produce and the import of timber from Scandinavia. Shipbuilding was also a significant trade here throughout the nineteenth century.

Isle of Whithorn's more recent sea-faring history has been darkened with tragedy. Seven local men perished in the sinking of the scallop dredger ***Solway Harvester*** on January 11 2000. The boat had been making its way towards shellfish beds off the coast of

Though still a fishing harbour, the Isle is also popular for yachting

north Wales when it hit stormy conditions and diverted for the shelter of Ramsay on the Isle of Man. It never made its destination, sinking so fast that there was no time to inflate the life-rafts. Three of the dead were from the Isle of Whithorn, all members of the Mills family: two brothers and their cousin. One of the brothers was actually a decorator by trade and, as a favour, had gone on the trip to fill-in for a crewman who was absent through sickness. Two months after his death his widow gave birth to their second child.

Of the other four victims, three were from Whithorn and one from Garlieston. A memorial made from Galloway granite was erected in 2004. Another granite memorial, overlooking Douglas Bay on the Isle of Man, was gifted 'to the Manx community in grateful thanks for their compassion and generosity'.

St Ninian's Chapel, contrary to popular supposition, is not where the fabled Christian missionary Ninian worshipped. This structure dates from the thirteenth century, some eight centuries after Ninian's reported death. Its closest possible association with the saint is more related to the subsequent veneration of his life. The chapel was probably used by pilgrims who arrived by sea on their way to the shrine at Whithorn and as a regular place of worship for the inhabitants of the immediate vicinity. The building was partly rebuilt towards the end of the nineteenth century. Much of the present stonework is therefore relatively modern. Parts of the earlier fabric were filched for private building work. It was reported

St Ninian's Chapel

The Witness Cairn with St Ninian's Chapel in the back-ground

in 1864 that a retired sea-captain 'took out the dressed stones some years ago to help up his house in the village'.

The tradition of pilgrimage to St Ninian's Chapel carries on to the present day and is very apparent in the **Witness Cairn**. Visitors place a votive offering of a stone. Many of these are painted with the names of loved ones.

Isle of Whithorn's '**castle**' is domestic rather than defensive, a laird's tower-house of the late seventeenth century. The remains of a fortified dwelling of much greater antiquity can be found at the south point of the peninsula: an Iron Age promontory **fort** at Isle Head.

The 'castle'

Kirkcolm

In the seventeenth century there was a burgh of barony here called Stewarton, but it had disappeared by the late eighteenth century when the building of the present village began. Ervie-Kirkcolm parish **kirk** was built in 1824. The birdcage bellcote is a twentieth-century concrete replacement.

The Celtic side of the Kilmorie Cross

The kirkyard has the ninth- or tenth-century **Kilmorie stone cross**. The cross is intriguing because the symbolic carvings on one side appear to be by a different hand from those on the opposite. One is Celtic in design, while the other has what may be Scandanavian influences. The cross has had a chequered existence. It came originally from the now extinct Kilmorie chapel, which was where the present St Mary's Croft is, due south of the village and by the west coast of Loch Ryan. Then it served for many years as a lintel in the former parish kirk. When that building became redundant, the cross was removed to the grounds of Corsewall House, north-east of the village. It was only in 1988 that it was brought to the present parish kirk.

Next to St Mary's Croft is **St Mary's Well**, of which the seventeenth-century Galloway chronicler Andrew Symson wrote:

> ...there is a well, to which people superstitiously resort, to fetch water for sick persones to drink; and they report, that if the person's disease be deadly, the well will be so dry, that it will be difficult to get water; but if the person be recoverable, then there will be water enough.

The plethora of local names incorporating Mary includes 'Kilmorie' itself, which is from Gaelic *cill*, 'church' and *Mhoiri*, 'Mary'.

With Kirkcolm having so many Christian associations, the Kirkcudbrightshire-based Baptist preacher David Gibson would naturally have expected a good turnout when he visited the village in

1814. It was not so, as he confided to his journal: 'In all the places I have been in Galloway, I have been well-received except in Kirkcolm.' When he returned two years later it looked as if the attitude remained the same: 'I was exceedingly disappointed to hear that the villagers were busy celebrating a wedding, so that no attention was likely to be paid to a sermon that evening.' He stuck it out till the following day, finally managed to get a hearing, and went away pretty pleased with himself: 'Afterwards several enquired if I would not come again.'

During the **Second World War** Kirkcolm hosted one of the county's military bases: the sea-plane maintenance depot at the bay to the south known as The Wig (see Part 2 - Wartime Wigtownshire). 'Wig' is from Norse *vik*, 'inlet'.

To the north-west of Kirkcolm, at the far end of the north Rhins peninsula, **Corsewall Lighthouse** was completed in 1816 to the design of Robert Stevenson, grandfather of the writer Robert Louis Stevenson. In its first few years the 86-ft tower was badly affected by damp. A coating of sand mixed in linseed oil eventually cured the problem. The light is now automated. The ancillary buildings have been converted into the Corsewall Lighthouse Hotel.

Corsewell Lighthouse

In 1898 Corsewall Point was the scene of a **shipwreck** reminiscent of the Compton Mackenzie novel/movie *Whisky Galore*. The *Firth of Cromarty*, on its way from Glasgow to Australia, was blown onto the rocks and wrecked, though the crew survived. The 2250 tons of cargo included a large consignment of whisky. It took a salvage team four days to reach the vessel and in the meantime much of the cargo had been washed ashore, greatly to the pleasure of the whisky-drinkers of Wigtownshire. 'Drunken parties took place on the shore wherever bottles or cases were found and one man was to later die of alcoholic poisoning due to his over-indulgence,' writes Peter C Miller, author of *Galloway Shipwrecks*, who himself found bottles of whisky during a diving expedition to the wreck in the 1970s.

At the time of the accident some salvaged supplies were buried underground for later use. There is reported still to be a cache of bottles hidden somewhere around Dally Bay further down the coast. Don't all go at once!

The remains of **Corsewall Castle** are to the south-east of the lighthouse. This rectangular tower-house of the Campbells of Corsewall dates probably from the fifteenth century.

Corsewall Castle

Due west of Kirkcolm, at the summit of Craigengerroch, the monument known as the **Marian Tower** is a bit of a puzzle. It is said to have been built in 1802, and the current assumption appears to be that it was erected by the Arctic explorer Sir John Ross in memory of his wife (see Part 2 - Celebrities of the Shire). Since Ross's wife did not die until 1822, this attribution cannot be correct. Nineteenth-century guide-books are more vague on the matter – wisely, it would seem. One merely mentions 'a Ross', while another goes no further than 'a fond husband'. Since the tower is adjacent to Balsarroch, the original Ross family home, it is likely to have been commissioned by a Ross, but almost certainly not by the famous Sir John.

The Marian Tower

Kirkcowan

Throughout the nineteenth century and into the twentieth, Kirkcowan's major source of employment was the handsome **waulk mill** by the banks of Tarf Water. Waulking is a method of making cloth thick and felted by soaking, beating and shrinking. Kirkcowan was a significant centre for the processing of wool from its moorland sheep. When the mill closed in 1950 it was still in the hands of the family who originally developed it, the Milroys, who built workers' accommodation in Milroy Terrace.

The now derelict Kirkcowan waulk mill and the burn that powered it

Kirkcowan has religious sites at both ends of the village. At the south is the now ruinous **old kirk** which had been completed in 1658. This was abandoned in 1834 in favour of the **new kirk**, with its striking forestair, at the north end of Main Street.

The village has the dubious distinction of having been missed by a famous travel writer. During a walking tour across Galloway in the summer of 1866 **George Borrow** was making his way from Glenluce to Newton Stewart. He was in need of food and drink around the time that he was in the vicinity of Kirkcowan, but he never got the sustenance that he was seeking:

> On this journey I intended to have passed through a place

> called Kirkcowan or something like it, but I followed the main road and passed by a cross road that leads to it...Kirkcowan was the only place where I could have gotten refreshments during a journey of 16 miles.

About this unfortunate aberration the local traveller and writer C H Dick commented somewhat waspishly half a century later:

> Borrow did not miss much when he left Kirkcowan unvisited, not even much in the way of a meal, so far as I have been able to judge. It seems to me a dull village, and the writer of *The Statistical Account* found remarkably little to say of the parish as a whole.

Travellers of a different kind, who never lost their way (though, when necessary, they could 'lose' themselves tactically), were the gangs of **smugglers** who frequented the former Thatch Inn during the eighteenth century. It was a convenient stopover as they transported their contraband from the Machars coastline to their customers in central Scotland.

The village has a claim to being the setting of Galloway's best-known poem ***The Brownie o' Blednoch*** by William Nicholson (1783-1849), 'Blednoch' being the nearby River Bladnoch. The poem is a racy tale of Aiken-drum, a supernatural being of awe-

Kirkcowan kirk

some ugliness ('there's a hole where a nose should hae been'), who suddenly appears in the neighbourhood, looking for work.

> I trow the bauldest stood aback,
> Wi' a gape and a glower till their lugs did crack,
> As the shapeless phantom mum'ling spak,
> 'Hae ye wark for Aiken-drum?'
>
> O! had ye seen the bairns' fright,
> As they stared at this wild and unyirthly wight,
> As he stauket in 'tween the dark and the light,
> And graned out, 'Aiken-drum!'

In 2005 a fine tradition of football in Kirkcowan came to an end after 131 years when **Tarff Rovers** left the field for the last time. Its most famous player, briefly in the late 1990s, had been Chic Charnley of Hibs and Partick Thistle. The club's final chairman described the fruitless calling of a public meeting: 'We put up posters in all the local pubs and on notice boards advertising the meeting but not a single person outside the committee turned up. The demography of Kirkcowan has made it impossible as the majority of people are of retiring age. We can hardly field a team with eighty-year-olds at the back and a ninety-year-old in goal.'

To the north-east of the village, **Shennanton House** is an English building in a Scottish setting. Completed in 1908, it was designed by H E Clifford (1852-1932) who, despite having a practice based in Glasgow, had a penchant for the styles of old England. He was an admirer of the 'Arts & Crafts' architect Norman Shaw who found inspiration for his country house designs in periods such as English Tudor. This is the manner that Clifford adopted for Shennanton, at a time when most architects north of the Border were reviving Scots Baronial.

Kirkinner

There used to be a quaint popular belief that the name meant 'Kirk-Inner'. The theory related to a time when the parish was much more extensive and the minister had to hold services in two kirks, one in the south and one in the north, which came to be referred to as Inner and Outer. So it was thought that the Inner became 'Kirkinner', while the Outer evolved into the later-created parish of Kirkcowan. Today's more scholarly etymology is '**Kirk of Kennera**'. St Kennera, according to a legend, was in a party of virgins heading for Rome. Most of them were massacred in Cologne. Kennera survived, only to be strangled with a napkin on the orders of the jealous wife of a Rhineland king who had taken a fancy to Kennera. Clearly, life in Cologne was more action-packed that it had been in Kirkinner.

The present **kirk** building dates from 1828 but the site was probably ecclesiastical long before that. A tenth-century Christian stone-carved cross, similar to some of those at the Whithorn Priory Museum, used to languish battered and broken in the kirkyard until the pieces were re-united and removed to the safety of the kirk interior. 'It is said by old people in the village [1890s] that a story has long been current in the district that parties when getting married joined hands in some way through the holes on the cross,' writes Malcolm Harper in *Rambles in Galloway*.

Kirkinner kirk

Between 1663 and 1686 the (Episcopalian) kirk minister was **Andrew Symson** (1638?-1712), whose *A Large Description of Galloway* is a key document for historical study of south-west Scotland in the seventeenth century. When he came to the parish from Edinburgh the circumstances were controversial. Kirk ministers dedicated to the purity of Presbyterianism were at that time being ousted from their posts and replaced by Episcopalian yes-men (see Part 2 – The Early History). Symson was one of the new incumbents, but his lack of bigotry appears to have made him as welcome as anyone could have been under those conditions. His account of Galloway life has vivid descriptions of farming methods and of local superstitions. After leaving Kirkinner he ended up back in Edinburgh as a publisher.

To the north of Kirkinner, **Milldriggan** is a significant piece of industrial archaeology. Its appearance is largely of the early-nineteenth century but this was a re-building of a much earlier mill. Milldriggan is believed to be one of the oldest continuous milling sites in south-west Scotland. After having been a woollen mill, it was converted to the processing of corn.

Milldriggan

Kirkmaiden

The name means '**kirk of St Medan**' and hereabouts it has a fourfold application: to the kirk on the hill, to the adjacent clachan, to the original kirk of Kirkmaiden close to the Mull of Galloway (see Drummore) and to the whole surrounding parish spread across the lower half of the south Rhins peninsula. Confusion is created by there also being a Kirkmaiden on the opposite side of Luce Bay. The two are sometimes differentiated thus: Kirkmaiden-in-Rhins and Kirkmaiden-in-Fernis (see Monreith).

Medan (or Medena) was, so the story goes, a beautiful Irish aristocrat of the eighth century. She was pestered by an over-zealous male admirer who, even after she had converted to Christianity and taken a vow of celibacy, would not take no for an answer. She fled across the sea and landed at Portankill on the west coast of Luce Bay just up from the Mull of Galloway. There she built a church, adapting a natural cave.

But her pious solitude was disturbed by the arrival of the love-struck stalker. She escaped from his clutches by taking refuge on a rock in the water. Lo and behold, the rock detached itself and carried her across the sea to Monreith Bay (see Monreith). However, it was not long before her admirer tracked her down to her new abode. This time she took refuge up a tree, from where she demanded to know why she was being persecuted in this way.

Interior of Kirkmaiden kirk

'Those eyes compel me,' he replied, whereupon Medan, never one for half-measures, tore out the said eyes. Then another miracle happened. A spring of healing water suddenly gushed from the ground and, after washing her damaged face in it, she recovered her sight. She resumed her work for Christ, while no doubt her traumatised suitor returned to Ireland for counselling.

As for the plausibility of St Medan's story, Galloway's great gentleman-antiquarian, Sir Herbert Maxwell of Monreith, is often quoted as a supporter of its truthfulness:

> There, on the sweep of strand before the church, lies the very rock which served Medana and her maids as a ferry-boat, just where they left it on landing; and there also the well bubbling cool and fresh from the rock, much venerated at this day as a wishing-well by lovers and other afflicted persons. To doubt the truth of the legend of St Medana is to disregard the plain evidence of one's senses.

Whenever Maxwell made that statement, he must surely have had his tongue in his cheek, for in his *The Place-Names of Galloway* he wrote of the legend: 'This is a fair example of the kind of farrago so often designed to explain the meaning of place-names.'

The present **kirk** of Kirkmaiden used to be called Kirk Covenant. That is because the building of it started in 1638, the year of the signing of the National Covenant against the royal imposition of Episcopalianism on the Church of Scotland.

In the kirkyard, the most striking memorial is in the shape of a lighthouse and was erected in the 1850s for a son of the Mull of Galloway lighthouse-keeper.

Lighthouse gravestone

North-west of Kirkmaiden village are the remains of **Clanyard Castle**, where a branch of the Gordons of Kenmure in Kirkcudbrightshire were installed from about 1500. One of the sixteenth-century Clanyard Gordons was particularly fearsome. He was so keen to win the affections of a neighbouring heiress that he had a rival suitor, a McDouall of Logan, killed. His murderous machismo still did not impress the young woman. More desirous of land than of love, he then abducted her father, hanging him by the thumbs over a steep cliff and forcing him to repeat:

> From me and from mine,
> To thee and to thine,
> The lands of Portcorkerie
> I forever resign.

At least that's how the story goes!

Only a small section of the wall of the castle still stands.

Kirkmaiden gets an honourable mention in the works of **Robert Burns**. In 1789 he was looking for a way of expressing the north-south extent of Scotland, ie from John o' Groats in the north-east corner of Caithness to Kirkmaiden, the southernmost parish of the land. But the stressed syllable in Kirkmaiden was in the wrong place for his scanning purposes. So he turned the name around, and this is how it appears in the first verse of *On the Late Captain Grose's Peregrinations*:

> Hear, Land o' Cakes, and brither Scots,
> Frae Maidenkirk to Johnny Groat's! –
> If there's a hole in a' your coats,
> I rede [warn] you tent [attend to] it:

> A chield's amang you takin' notes,
> And, faith, he'll prent it.

Did the folk of the parish have a reputation for ingenuity in avoiding tiresome tasks? According to the *Dictionary of the Scots Language*, a **Kirkmaiden patch** is 'a handful of straw stuffed in a hole in a corn sack to save darning it'.

Leswalt

A village associated with the Agnew stronghold of **Lochnaw Castle** to its west. The original core of the castle is a tower-house built in the fifteenth or sixteenth century. This was added to at three different periods up to the nineteenth century. The two later stages of re-building were removed around 1950. The ruins of a much older castle are on the small island in Lochnaw Loch. During the Second World War, the castle was turned into a temporary military hospital (see Part 2 - Wartime Wigtownshire).

Lochnaw Castle

The **Agnews** were eminent figures in Wigtownshire affairs for many centuries. The most popular theory about their origins is that they were French Normans from the Barony d'Agneaux. They may have reached Galloway via Ireland. 'Agneaux' is presumed to have evolved into 'Agnew'.

They first came to prominence in Wigtownshire in 1426 when Andrew Agnew was created Constable of Lochnaw. The family's greatest claim to fame in the history of the county is that for some three hundred years they were the Hereditary Sheriffs. This anomalous post, passed from father to son across twelve generations, was finally abolished in 1747 (see Part 2 – The Early History).

Despite the loss of their judicial status the Agnews continued to be big players in the politics of the county. A dynasty that had earlier produced one or two dubious characters had become, by the eighteenth century, terribly respectable. Sir Andrew Agnew (1793-1849) was a leading Sabbatarian. As MP for Wigtownshire, he piloted a Lord's Day Observance bill through Parliament and might have got it passed had he not lost his seat in 1837.

Andrew Agnew, author of *The Hereditary Sheriffs of Galloway*

His son, also Andrew (1818-1892), wrote a classic history of the family, *The Hereditary Sheriffs of Galloway* (a slightly misleading title, since their jurisdiction did not extend into the separate Stewartry of Kirkcudbright). And *his* son, [Andrew] Noel, is the one who in 1892 commissioned John Singer Sargent's swanky portrait *Lady Agnew of Lochnaw* (see below). Noel, like his father, took up the pen and compiled the little-known but commendably workmanlike *Wigtownshire – A Guide for Visitors* (1908). His own family history could not be ignored in the book. About the coming to an end of the long line of his forbears as Hereditary Sheriffs, he writes without sentimentality: '...the Agnews, who had maintained order and administered justice in the County for twelve generations, made way for a more modern system.'

During the twentieth century the Agnew family gradually lost its direct landed connection with Lochnaw. Noel and his wife had no children. In 1928 his nephew Sir Fulque Agnew (1900-75) inherited the title, but little else. Fulque and his wife, the redoubtable Swanzie Erskine, spent much of their lives in Africa, he working as a university administrator, she becoming Professor of Geography at the University of Malawi. While working in white-controlled South Africa, they fell foul of the authorities for their opposition to apartheid. When Swanzie died in 2001, the *Daily Telegraph* obituary summed her up as the 'roving wife of an itinerant baronet' ('roving' is a reference to travels rather than to marital infidelities!). In 2001 a selection of Sir Fulque's letters was published as *Witness to the Partition: India and Pakistan 1947-48*. Fulque and Swanzie's only son, Sir Crispin Agnew, 11th baronet, became a senior officer at the Court of the Lord Lyon, Scotland's arbitrator on all matters heraldic.

Lady Agnew of Lochnaw
John Singer Sargent

Lady Agnew of Lochnaw (1892) by John Singer Sargent (1856-1925) is now one of the most popular paintings at the National Gallery in Edinburgh. In 1889 at St Peter's, Eaton Square in London, Gertrude Vernon married Sir [Andrew] Noel Agnew, 9th baronet. He was 39, she was 24. She had earlier turned him down but he continued pursuing her and it is said that, when they finally did marry, she was not in love with him. She was often mysteriously sickly, and that was sometimes the excuse for not accompanying her husband to his Lochnaw estate; they spent substantial periods of their married life apart.

The year in which Noel commissioned the portrait is noteworthy: that was when his father died and Noel at last got his inheritance. The choice of the American Sargent was quite daring. The artist had recently left Paris under a cloud, his portrait of *Madame X* having been considered indecent because of the provocative positioning of a shoulder-strap.

Gertrude Vernon

However, when Gertrude's picture went on view at the Royal Academy in 1893 it stole the show. The critics raved, as they did again when it had a second London showing the following year at the Grafton Galleries in an exhibition called *Fair Women*. For both artist and sitter life changed considerably. Sargent's career took off: he became an Associate of the Royal Academy in 1894, a full Academician in 1897. Gertrude, meanwhile, became famous as a society beauty, though, judging from the only extant photograph of her, the artist had perhaps slightly enhanced her looks.

By the 1920s the Agnew fortune was diminishing, allegedly because of Gertrude's spending habits. In 1924 she opened negotiations with the National Gallery over the possibility of their purchasing the picture. Claiming that otherwise it would be sold more profitably to an American collector, she offered the gallery a special price:

> ...I am obliged to sell it – and of course £4,000 is the lowest figure I can offer it for...Of course the matter is entirely confidential as that is not a figure I should entertain if sold elsewhere.

At the time Sargent was still alive and the gallery initially declined the offer because of their policy of not buying work by living artists. However, after Sargent died in 1925 the deal was done.

When Gertrude died in 1932 her obituary in the *Times* said:

> Many are the friends who will cherish the memory of that handsome figure, with the glorious dark eyes of wisdom, and the enchanting voice, which combined so perfectly emphasis with harmony.

In Leswalt itself the ruins of the medieval **kirk**, at the west end of the village, contain an Agnew burial vault. The replacement kirk, at the east end, was built in the late 1820s.

To the north-west of the village, at Tor of Craigoch, there is a **monument** to Sir Andrew Agnew, who died in 1849. For this purpose the Agnews rather presumptuously appropriated the site of an Iron Age **hill-fort**.

The Agnew Monument

Galdenoch Castle

Further to the west of Leswalt, beyond Lochnaw, is another former Agnew stronghold, **Galdenoch Castle**, built in the middle of the sixteenth century. Most tower-houses of this period are associated with a ghost, but the **Ghost of Galdenoch** is unusually appealing because it had a sense of humour. Generations of the castle's inhabitants were tormented by the tricks that the spirit played upon them. The spinner's threads would be mysteriously severed and lumps of peat would appear in the porridge. The ghost's finest hour came with its abduction of an elderly woman, as related by Sir Andrew Agnew in his family history:

> Great was the surprise of the family at dinner-time when grandmamma was missed. Every corner of the building was searched. The goodman and his wife became alarmed, while the lads and lassies ran madly about interrogating one another with 'Where's granny?' At last a well-known voice was heard – 'I've washed granny in the burn, and laid her on the dyke to dry!' Away the whole party ran; and sure enough the poor old woman lay naked on the dyke, half dead with cold and fright.

One ghost-buster after another had no success in ridding the castle of the spectral pest till finally along came the Rev Marshall from Kirkcolm, 'a zealous prosecutor of witches'. His method was simple: he out-talked it (not a difficult task for a Presbyterian minister). The exorcism endured throughout the night:

> Faint gleams of light streaked the eastern horizon, when an unearthly voice, husky and weak, whined, 'Roar awa', Marshall, I can roar nae mair!' Marshall still continued, determined to make assurance doubly sure; but the ghost kept his word and was never heard again.

On the Rhins shore south-west of Galdenoch, **Salt Pans Bay** is a reminder of a small-scale but vital rural industry that was once so important for the preservation of meat and fish for both domestic consumption and export. The salt pans here were carved into the rocks, collecting sea water that was then evaporated. Production of Galdenoch salt is thought to have begun in the 1630s and lasted until the early nineteenth century.

Lochans

A 'lochan' is of course a small loch. The plural suggests that there must have been more evidence of water around here before Wigtownshire's agriculture moved into a period of intensive improvement from the early eighteenth century onwards. Drainage was one of the components of this radical transformation of the landscape (see Part 2 – The Land and the Sea).

Lochans lies along the Piltanton Burn which had to be crossed when the **railway** system was extended from Stranraer to Portpatrick in the early 1860s. The engineering solution was a spectacular whinstone-and-brick bridge, sometimes known as the Lochans Viaduct. It was demolished in the 1980s. The village did not benefit from having its own station. The nearest halt was placed well to the south-west at **Colfin**, which in the 1860s was pretty deserted. But the Colfin halt became more directly useful when a creamery was built beside it in 1919, and, although the rail link to Portpatrick was discontinued in 1950, the Colfin-Stranraer section was kept open to service the milk-supply chain for another nine years.

The former creamery building is now the **Colfin Smokehouse**, whose range of fish products extends far beyond the usual salmon and trout. The fish is prepared in a solution of salt-water, brown sugar and dark rum and then smoked over oak sawdust from old whisky casks. But can even that procedure manage to make *eel* appetising?

Mochrum

Formerly known as Kirk of Mochrum. The **kirk** was built in 1794 and still has its original pulpit. The manse of the same period was expanded in 1822 and again in 1900-1.

At the north-east end of the village, **Druchtag Motte** is a fine example of the twelfth-century 'pudding-shaped' type of earthwork, on which there would have been a timber-built castle.

Despite its name **Old Place of Mochrum** is far away from the village, to the north-west by Mochrum Loch. Some of it is very old; the rest is early-twentieth-century. Originally there were two separate tower-houses, one of the fifteenth century, the other of the sixteenth. By the nineteenth century they were both ruinous. Their owner, the 3rd Marquess of Bute (1847-1900), who was an obsessive medievalist, embarked on a massive restoration from 1873, adding a hall that linked the two towers. After his death, the 4th Marquess carried on the work, creating whole new ranges to the north and east and fitting out the interiors in the 'Arts and Crafts' style. The result, according to a modern architectural historian, is a 'house of almost magical appeal'.

The **Dunbars** were the original occupants of Old Place of Mochrum as it was in the fifteenth century. The most famous of the family was Gavin Dunbar (died 1547) who was tutor to the future King James V, archbishop of Glasgow and Lord Chancellor of

Old Place of Mochrum

Scotland. Earlier Dunbars are thought to have lived in an island fortification within Castle Loch to the west of Old Place of Mochrum. A seventeenth-century Dunbar, Sir James, was so big that he was virtually a giant, and so anything outsize was sometimes described as a 'mochrum'.

Folk of this parish used to be nicknamed by others '**Mochrum scarts**'. *Scart* (or *scaurt*) is an old Galloway Scots word for 'cormorant'. The phrase was inspired by the proliferation of cormorants on Castle Loch. For their part the cormorants were sometimes referred to as 'Mochrum elders' (the birds and the kirk officers both being in black). In his *Scottish Gallovidian Encyclopedia* (1824) John Mactaggart had another phrase for the cormorants. Calling them 'Mochrum lairds', he said it was 'because they have been, as it were, proprietors there of a piece of wild shore, for an *unknown* length of time'.

'Mochrum Elders'

Monreith

A village and an estate long associated with the **Maxwells**, including Galloway's grand old man of letters Sir Herbert Maxwell and his writer grandson Gavin Maxwell, best known for *Ring of Bright Water* (see Part 2 - The Writers). It used to have a longer name, Milltown of Monreith, there having been grain mills powered by the Monreith Burn. In the early nineteenth century, when major agrarian improvements were taking place across the county, the demand for drainage tiles led to the creation here of a **brick and tile works**, owing to the local presence of clay.

It was the MacCullochs who originally held sway here. Their stronghold was **Myrton Castle** which is now within the Monreith estate. A timber tower atop a twelfth-century motte was replaced around 1500 by a stone version and this was added to in the early seventeenth century. King James IV used Myrton when he visited the shrine of St Ninian at Whithorn. The Maxwells took over Myrton later in the seventeenth century and then in the 1790s began the building of the present **Monreith House**. Sir Herbert described how that came about:

> My great-grandfather, having to go and attend to his parliamentary duties in London, left with his wife £2,000 to make an addition to the old castle in which they lived. In what seems to us now an evil moment she listened to the advice

Monreith House

Sir Herbert Maxwell

> of an architect who, as she reported to her husband in a letter still in my possession, persuaded her that he could erect on a fresh site 'a much more genteel residence' than the old one. Sir William having raised no objection, the central block of the present house was built in part, but the wings were never begun.

Gavin Maxwell commented tartly:

> In order to build the genteel residence this vandal of an architect pulled down the greater part of Myrton Castle, leaving, by the time he had finished carting stone to the new site, little but the tower and the great walled garden; so that the glorious avenue of beeches led only to ruins and nettles.

Around 1870 Myrton Castle was converted into a doocot.

According to Gavin Maxwell, his ancestors 'avoided fame but not always notoriety, the peculiar wickedness of certain holders of the title being documented with scurrilous detail in the parish records.' He claimed that the worst of them 'had a black page boy whom he beat to death, and a white horse on which he went wenching at night, wandering far afield like a tomcat and leaving not a few unacknowledged kittens'.

These ancestors included John Maxwell, a prominent fighter on behalf of the Covenanters in their struggle to prevent the Episcopalian takeover of Scotland in the seventeenth century (he was succeeded in the title by an Episcopalian!) Another Maxwell, who was a wily gambler, wagered a rival that from the top of the nearby Fell of Barhullion you could see five kingdoms. They climbed to the summit and agreed that the ancient kingdoms of Scotland, England, Ireland and Mann [Isle of Man] were in view. But that was only four. The fifth? 'Look aboon ye, man – there's the kingdom of Heaven, and maybe ye'll never be nearer it.'

Monreith House is beside the **White Loch of Myrton**. The water was reputed to have both bleaching and therapeutic properties. Towards the south end of the loch there is evidence of a prehistoric **crannog**, a tribal home on an artificial island.

Old Place of Monreith, to the north-east, is an earlier Maxwell residence, a tower-house of about 1600. Also known as Dowies, it

Old Place of Monreith, also known as 'Dowies'

has been restored by the Landmark Trust, the preservation charity that makes its properties available for holiday lets. One renter left this rhyming observation in the visitors' book: 'The Old Place of Monreith/ Is not suitable for people called Sharon or Keith.'

For the family mausoleum the Maxwells of Monreith chose the ancient chapel of **Kirkmaiden-in-Fernis**, part of a holy site of great antiquity and beguiling charm close to Monreith Bay. The chapel is dedicated to St Medan, since this is where she is supposed to have escaped to in trying to avoid her suitor (see Kirkmaiden). Part of the medieval fabric was restored towards the end of the nineteenth century and turned into the mausoleum. The

Kirkmaiden-in-Fernis

famous tenth-century carving known as the **Monreith Cross**, which for generations sat in the garden of Monreith House, is thought to have come originally from here. It is now kept safely at the Whithorn Priory Museum.

Along the shoreline rocks slightly to the north-west of the chapel is the reputed site of **St Medan's Well** (where, according to the legend, she bathed her damaged eyes). This used to be alternatively known as Chincough [whooping cough] Well, as the water was once believed to be a cure for the ailment.

The Thurot plaque

St Medan's kirkyard is the burial-place of the infamous French privateer and sometime smuggler **François Thurot**, whose body was washed ashore here in 1760. During the Seven Years' War of 1756-63, which brought France and Britain into conflict, Thurot and his crew were causing mischief around the Irish Sea when they were challenged by a British fleet off the north coast of the Isle of Man. Thurot was killed by a cannonball. When his body, which had been thrown into the sea, came ashore at Monreith Bay, it was identified from the clothing. His grave was not marked. In the 1860s an antiquarian with a special interest in Thurot reminisced:

> In 1812 or 1813 I happened to be at Port William, and on my expressing a wish to visit it, the spot was pointed out to me as traditionally known to be the grave of Thurot. It was scarcely distinguishable from the narrow mounds around it; but it must still be known and respected, for until lately, and perhaps even now, the memory of the daring deeds of Thurret (thus his name was pronounced) was preserved and extolled in Gallovidian song.

A memorial plaque for Thurot was placed here in 1960. Describing him as 'gallant', it states that 'he introduced the Ancient Order of Coldin [a mariners' secret society] to Sweden' and that it was this organisation that put up the plaque.

At the top of the cliffs here there is a **Gavin Maxwell memorial**: predictably enough, a sculpture of an otter (see Part 2 – The Writers).

Gavin Maxwell memorial

The area to the north-east of Monreith is rich in examples of what are referred to as **cup-and-ring markings**, rock carvings of the second millennium BC, the explanation for which archaeologists are still not agreed upon (see Part 2 – The Early History).

Barsalloch Point, on the coast to the west of Monreith, is the site of a chieftain's fort of the last millenium BC. Its general shape, with defensive ditch and ramparts, is still apparent.

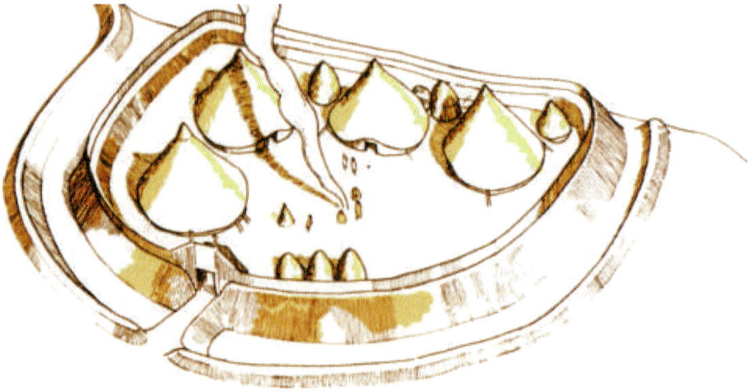

Artist's impression of what Barsalloch Fort might have looked like

New Luce

Part of New Luce from the bridge over the River Luce

The village takes its name from the parish. In the middle of the seventeenth century the original parish stretching along the whole of the Luce valley was divided into two, more manageable units: Old Luce (centred on Glenluce) and New Luce. The village grew naturally where the Cross Water of Luce meets the Main Water of Luce.

From 1659 New Luce's minister was **Alexander Peden**, a star preacher among the Covenanters (see Part 2 – The Early History). Not for nothing was he known as 'Peden the Prophet'. He had a mesmeric style of oratory, by which his parishioners were awestruck. Intolerant and self-righteous, he had a nasty habit of predicting death for anyone who did not accept the tenets of his own militant beliefs. Refusing to accept Episcopalianism, he was ousted from his post in 1662. His farewell sermon was particularly dramatic. Lasting until midnight, it finally came to an end with Peden's symbolic barring of the door against any usurping successor.

Peden continued his preaching in the open-air conventicles to which the persecuted Covenanters had to resort. With his renown spreading, he became a marked man, as a result of which he fled to Ireland. On his return he was arrested, put on trial and imprisoned on the Bass Rock in the Firth of Forth. Later he was sentenced to transportation to Virginia but, having got only as far as London, he was set free after the ship's captain refused to carry anyone convicted for his religious principles. Returning to Scotland, he led a wandering existence until he died in his native Ayrshire in 1686. In 1682 he had returned briefly to New Luce and preached two sermons which were published posthumously as *The Lord's Trumpet Sounding an Alarm*.

In 1871 when a Free kirk was opened in New Luce, it was named after Peden. That building has since been demolished. The present **parish kirk** was built in 1821.

Thanks to the **railways**, New Luce once had easy access to the outside world. When the Girvan and Portpatrick Junction Railway opened in 1877, there were stations at both New Luce and Glenwhilly to the north, until their closure in 1965. The line remains open for the service between Stranraer and Ayr. Passing trains that no longer stop here are a taunting reminder of a lost facility.

The hill and moorland country surrounding New Luce abounds in **standing stones** and **cairns**, all largely of the second or third millennium BC. A number of the most interesting examples lie just off the Southern Upland Way as it snakes its way north-eastwards from New Luce, in particular the burial chambers at Caves of Kilhern and at Cairn na Gath.

Even further to the north-east are the stones at **Laggangarn**. Thousands of years after they were erected, possibly in the eighth century, Christian propagandists carved crosses onto them. It is traditionally said that originally there were up to thirteen stones, the missing ones having been used for building work. In the 1870s an archaeologist reported on the apparent consequences of abusing them:

> A man, M'Millan, tenant of the farm about 100 years ago, used several for lintels in the new buildings he erected. Soon after he was bitten by a mad dog, which he caught by the tail as it was going in at the dog-hole in the house-door, and brained it against the door cheek. He took hydrophobia, and, at his own request, was smothered under a feather-bed in a paroxysm of his disease! In the following autumn his sister-in-law, who had helped to smother him, slipped on some frozen straw in the barnyard, and suffered compound fracture of an arm, of which she died. The neighbours looked on these deaths as judgments for the

desecration of the 'stanin stanes'. Let all greedy builders take warning!

Laggangarn standing stones

The same remote countryside has deposits of **lead**. At Knockibae, north of the village, it was mined intermittently during the eighteenth and nineteenth centuries.

Newton Stewart

It is not surprising that a settlement developed along this stretch of the **River Cree**. It was here that the river could be forded and so from earliest times numerous land trading-routes converged at this spot. It was a particularly important crossing-point for the 'droving' of cattle towards the markets of England (see Part 2 – The Land and the Sea).

The river was also a long-accepted jurisdictional and administrative dividing-line (see Introduction). Older residents still remember the effects of the two counties of Galloway having different alcohol licensing hours. Wigtownshire's watering-holes remained open half an hour later at night than those in Kirkcudbrightshire. When it was 'time, gentlemen, please!' in Minnigaff and Creebridge on the Stewartry side, there was a drinkers' dash across the Bridge of Cree into the boozers of Newton Stewart.

It was in fact the east bank of the Cree that burgeoned first. Minnigaff had a kirk and a cattle market long before 1677 when the **'new town' of Stewart** was created a burgh of barony on the west bank (Minnigaff is now but a suburb of its former rival). The local patrons were the Stewart family, holders of the earldom of Galloway. It was William Stewart, son of the 2nd earl, who instigated its 1677 burghal recognition. However, development did not get properly underway until the early 1700s. Till then Newton Stewart's west bank consisted of little more than a single property, Ford House of Cree.

Later in the eighteenth century the patronage of the gentry gave way to the mercantile zeal of a local upstart **William Douglas** (1745-1809). From relatively humble beginnings in the parish of Penninghame Douglas rose to entrepreneurial eminence as a merchant in Glasgow, London and north America. He eventually returned home to Galloway and lavished his wealth on becoming a laird. After strenuous lobbying he finally got his knighthood but, despite allocating a substantial budget to the business of bribing the right connections, Sir William failed to get the peerage he craved.

William Douglas

One of Sir William's first acts on acquiring the Stewart estate was a somewhat egotistical change of name to Newton *Douglas*. With great plans for the area joining in the Industrial Revolution, he set up a **cotton** factory but in the long-term it was not a success and the building was demolished in 1826. Having failed to realise his dream of a Creeside cottonopolis, Douglas concentrated his later efforts on developing the town of Castle Douglas in Kirkcudbrightshire. Though his name lived on there, his business retreat from the Shire saw 'Newton Douglas' revert back to 'Newton Stewart'.

Along the Cree the move from fording to bridging was crucial to the town's attempts at development during the eighteenth century. The first bridge, of 1745, was washed away in 1806 and replaced in 1813 by the present **Cree Bridge**, a handsome granite structure designed by the eminent engineer John Rennie. Upstream, the pedestrian suspension bridge was built in 1911 to mark the coronation of King George V. Another pedestrian bridge, the Sparling, was constructed downstream in 1998. A river that can be forded is of course never going to be deep enough for berthing facilities: the nearest Newton Stewart ever got to having a harbour was a couple of miles downstream at **Carty Port**.

Nineteenth-century Newton Stewart settled snugly into its role as a **market town** for the surrounding countryside. Its industrial en-

Newton Stewart Town Hall

terprises were small-scale and ancillary to the region's agriculture: there were grain mills; wool from Shire sheep went into the manufacture of clothing and carpets; a tannery processed local cattle hides; pigs ended up in the bacon-curing factory. In 1899 Cree Mills began making tweed and other woollen products on the site of the original short-lived cotton factory. By the 1950s it was employing some 150 people but it closed in 1986.

The old Cotton Mill Row was re-named King Street, and another stretch known as the Gorbals became Arthur Street. In a kind of roll-call of British patriotism, the long thoroughfare from north to south through the town continues with Victoria Street, Albert Street and Queen Street. In Victoria Street the **Town Hall** was built around 1800, and where the roadway widens out to the south of the town hall was the original market-place. The modern **livestock mart**, towards the end of Queen Street, has a distinctive octagonal auction-ring, built in 1894. Another imposing public building is at the point where Albert Street turns into Queen Street: the **McMillan Hall** of 1884, named after the McMillan sisters, a couple of spinsters who bequeathed money for the building of it.

Meanwhile, the **railways** had reached the town by the 1860s (and departed again a century later). Newton Stewart station lay on the cross-Galloway Portpatrick Railway, and a decade later it also became the northern terminus of the Wigtownshire Railway that went south to Whithorn (see Part 2 – The Land and the Sea). Rail communication not only boosted commerce but also brought recreational visitors to the area. The increasing popularity of the town as a tourism base revitalised old coaching-inns like the eighteenth-century **Galloway Arms Hotel** in Victoria Street, not to mention the thirty-four pubs that the town once had.

In the early 1900s the Galloway novelist **S R Crockett**, mindful of the town's picturesque and historic hinterland, described Newton Stewart as 'the natural gateway and distributing point for much enchanted ground'. The town certainly seems to have cast an enchantment in the early 1930s upon the English travel writer

H V Morton of *In Search of Scotland* and *In Scotland Again* fame. Morton may momentarily have lost his sense of proportion, for, bonnie as it is, the view from the Cree Bridge would not bring to mind for many people thoughts of *La Serenissima* of the Aegean Sea: 'the old houses...drop straight down to the water exactly as houses do in Venice'.

Morton was struck by how quiet the town seemed:

> ...a clean, swept and garnished little town which even on weekdays has an atmosphere of the Sabbath about it. It reminds me of those small-scale models which you sometimes see on an architect's table, abnormally neat and tidy and clear-cut. Someone in Newton Stewart has set an inhuman standard of cleanliness and integrity to which the town faithfully adheres. At least that is my impression.

The open space onto which the McMillan Hall fronts used to be familiarly known as the Angle but its official name is **Dashwood Square**. In 1764 the 7th Earl of Galloway married an Anne Dashwood. Their children offer excellent examples of how the younger male scions of aristocratic families used to find a purpose in life given the fact that they were unlikely to inherit the father's title. The usual outlets were the military and the clerical, and that is the pattern followed by the second and third surviving Galloway/Dashwood boys. **William Stewart** (1774-1827) became a distinguished general. He was the founder of the Rifle Brigade and became a close friend of Nelson, after whom he named his son Horatio. During service in the Napoleonic wars Stewart was affectionately known to his men as 'auld grog Willie' because of the extra rations of rum he allowed them

The McMillan Hall

(though Wellington made him foot the bill for his liberality). After seventeen campaigns and numerous injuries, ill-health forced him to retire to Minnigaff, where he built the hunting-lodge at Cumloden. General Stewart had lived up to the family motto *Virescit vulnere virtus*, 'valour grows strong from a wound'.

General Stewart's younger brother Charles was the one who entered the church, having been much influenced in childhood by an evangelical minister who was one of his private tutors. The Rev Stewart went to Canada as a missionary in 1807 and in 1826 was appointed Bishop of Quebec. He remained in Canada until shortly before his death in 1837.

A **monument** at the west end of the Cree Bridge commemorates another Earl of Galloway: Randolph, the 9th (1800-1873). It was erected the year after his death and describes him as 'a generous landlord, munificent in charity, a sincere humble-minded Christian, and noble and worthy example to posterity'. True to the Galloway appellation, he was at one time Lord Lieutenant of *both* Wigtownshire and Kirkcudbrightshire, though when he served in Parliament it was as the representative for the town of Cockermouth in Cumberland.

The Galloway **earldom** was created for the Stewarts by King James VI and I in 1623. The family's original strongholds had been **Garlies Castle**, to the north-east of the town, and **Castle Stewart**, to the north-west. Both were built in the early part of the sixteenth century. The zenith of the earldom's power and prestige was expressed in the magnificence of Galloway House, built in the Machars during the 1740s (see Garlieston). By the early 1900s the family could no longer afford the upkeep of their grand seat and transferred to the more modest house at Cumloden which had been built for General William Stewart (see above).

Castle Stewart

Three and a half centuries after the Galloway lineage was established it all went horribly wrong, as became apparent when the 12th Earl died in 1978. Lord Galloway had always been embarrassed by the social and intellectual inadequacies of his

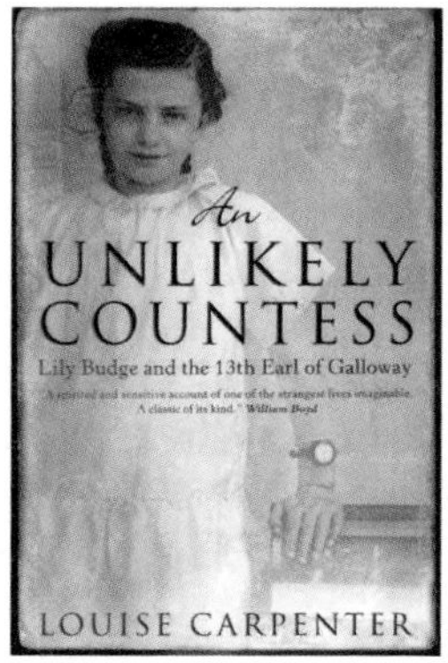

schizophrenic son and heir Randolph (born 1928). When Randolph married a working-class Borders woman called Lily Budge, his father was so convinced that she was a fortune-seeker that he disinherited his son. Randolph junior duly succeeded as the 13th Earl (no one could legally deprive him of that) but the keys to Cumloden were handed over to a distant relative. The whole sorry tale is told by Louise Carpenter in *An Unlikely Countess* (2004).

The name of the town's **Douglas-Ewart High School** maintains recognition of two philanthropic educational endowments of the nineteenth century, whose buildings have now been adapted to other purposes. The earliest was the Douglas Free School in King Street, which was opened in 1834. Thirty years later came the Ewart Institute in York Road. The two schools were amalgamated in the 1920s. The high school's present premises in Corsbie Road have been built in stages since the 1960s.

A former pupil of the Douglas-Ewart now holds a Nobel Prize for economics. At school **James Mirrlees** (born 1936) explored books while others played football. 'By the age of fourteen I had acquired a strange enthusiasm for mathematics, having managed to acquire a book called *Teach Yourself Calculus*, and done so'. He has been an economics professor at both Oxford and Cambridge universities. The Nobel honour was awarded in 1996, and in the following year he received a knighthood. In *Who's Who* he describes his main recreation, teasingly, as 'reading detective stories and other forms of mathematics'.

Other distinguished products of a Newton Stewart schooling included the Chartist leader **Peter McDouall** and the veterinary scientist **John McFadyean** (see Part 2 – Celebrities of the Shire).

A town is always enhanced by being the headquarters of a newspaper and since 1870 Newton Stewart has enjoyed that status thanks to the ***Galloway Gazette***. Previously the main source of local information had been the *Wigtown Free Press and Stranraer Advertiser*, established in 1843. The founding of the *Gazette* not only ensured better coverage of the eastern part of the Shire but also offered a more Conservative viewpoint to counteract the then Liberal bias of the *Free Press*.

The *Galloway Gazette* has had fewer editors in its history than most newspapers because one twentieth-century incumbent, J F

Brown, occupied the post for fifty-seven years. His successor, J Ridley Brown, was always keen to provide unusual features. In the 1950s he commissioned comic sketches from the coal-miner turned playwright and poet **Joe Corrie** (1894-1968). Though reared in Fife, Corrie knew the Shire well through family connections. 'No matter how poor we were when I was a boy,' he recalled, 'there was always my train-fare from Fife to Newton Stewart when the school holidays came round. Once in Newton Stewart Galloway kindness provided the rest'. One of Corrie's funniest stories was about the postman-poet Hamish McClure:

> Hamish is yin o' the poetic sowls wha doesna look it. He has nae hair left on his pate; his nose is on the big size to fit his face properly, and due to many years in the service o' the Post Office, his feet are as flat as flounders. But, despite his poetic weakness, he's no' a bad sowl. So we decided to ha'e a leisurely walk alang the banks o' the Cree, which, in Hamish's ain words, contains a maisterpiece o' poetry at every bend.
>
> It was indeed a gem o' a mornin'; there was hardly a cloud in the sky, and the birds were liltin' cheerily. Hamish was in his usual meditative mood, and I didna disturb him; just puffed awa' at my pipe and thoucht aboot naething.

Newton Stewart Museum

> Then Hamish came to a sudden stop, and said, wi' his hand to his lug, "Hark! A lark!" So he took his notebook frae his pooch, stuck his pencil in his mooth, and sat doon on a tree stump to record his inspiration...He feenished his poem in aboot five minutes – it never tak's him lang – and when he got up on his feet he says to me, "Tam, ye can aye say in future years that you was wi' me when I wrote the maisterpiece 'The Lark Abune the Cree'." I said I was highly honoured, just to please him.

Two examples of architectural renewal stand out in the Newton Stewart of today. An 1880s former kirk in York Road was turned into the local **museum** in 1978.

In Victoria Street the characteristically 1920s **cinema** has been refurbished and, against the odds for a town of this size, is kept going through community ownership. The films it shows include the very latest releases.

The Cinema

Port Logan

It was originally known as **Port Nessock** but, as Robert Trotter put it in *Galloway Gossip* (1878), 'like a great many places in Galloway it has turned genteel and changed its name'. As ever, the replacement name was in homage (or more plausibly self-homage) to the local gentry, in this case the McDoualls of Logan. Port Logan was developed as their estate village in the early nineteenth century.

Once upon a time there were high hopes for the expansion of this tiny place into a major **port**. It was a serious rival to Portpatrick and Stranraer as the main terminal for the Irish Sea traffic. As early as the 1680s it was reported that the laird 'hath been at

The port at Port Logan

great paines and expences to build a port'. In 1715 a government surveyor, tasked with identifying the most suitable harbour site on the Rhins, concluded that the bay here was the only feasible option. Another assessment was undertaken in 1809 by the civil engineer John Rennie. He recommended the building of a pier, a lighthouse and a sea-wall. From 1818 Colonel Andrew McDouall had most of the proposals carried out and for a time the port thrived on importing Irish cattle. The circular granite lighthouse was added at the end of the pier in the 1830s. However, the harbour thereafter went into decline.

Robert Trotter speculated about Port Logan's failure to flourish: 'there was a rock at the pier head that the contractors neglected to blast out, and the Colonel made them blast it after the pier was finished, and they did it in such a way that it shook the pier to pieces and spoiled the harbour. He went to law with them, but to no purpose except spending a lot of money.' Trotter asserts that 'it might have made a splendid harbour by putting a breakwater across the mouth of the bay; and if half the money had been spent on it that was wasted over Portpatrick, it would have been one of the finest harbours in the West of Scotland.'

One of Colonel McDouall's pet schemes lasted, though, and is now the village's most striking feature, the **fish pond**. In 1788 McDouall had the idea of using a natural rock formation as a larder for fish brought in by the tides. He spent the next twelve years converting it. McDouall was particularly keen on cod for his table. The fish were famously tame, a phenomenon observed in 1831 by the itinerant preacher David Gibson: 'The large codfish allow you to stroke their heads, and take meat out of your hand. I saw some of the little fish, which did not put their heads above the waters as others did, take food out of the hand when the hand was under water.'

An Edwardian journalist reported that many of the older cod were blind:

The Fish Pond, Port Logan

> ...for many years it was imagined that the cause of this must be the comparative shallowness of the water, the cod being a deep-sea fish...This, however, is not the reason, for it has lately been ascertained that when several fish together make a dash at the same morsel of food, they often inadvertently scratch one another's eyes with their needle-like teeth, thus injuring them, and ultimately causing blindness.

Nineteenth-century Port Logan had a massive **herring fishery**. The travel illustrator William Daniell wrote about what he saw in 1815: 'An animated scene here presented itself, there being in the bay about an hundred and fifty sail of boats on the herring fishery, each boat manned with from five to eight men'.

After the decline of the fishing fleet, herring were still being caught around Port Logan until the second half of the twentieth century by an unorthodox method known as 'jigging'. In the mid-1950s the parish minister described the technique in great detail:

> Two thin metal spars (the spokes of old umbrellas are much favoured), about ten inches long, are bound together to make a cross, which is attached by its centre near the end of a weighted line, and two more such crosses are placed at short intervals above that; unbaited hooks are attached at each of the twelve ends of the spars. In the summer evenings, when the shoals of herring come into the bay, the fishers go out in rowing boats with these 'jigs' and try to come amongst the fish, when the whole contraption is dropped into the shoal and jigged up and down by means of the line; if the shoals are packed tight, large quantities of fish are caught up on these twelve hooks.

In 1867 the sea yielded a bumper catch for Port Logan's boozers thanks to a **shipwreck**. A barque by the name of *Strathleven* was returning to Greenock from Demerara in South America when disaster struck and its cargo of rum was disgorged. As rumours of the rum spread across the Rhins, many a farmer downed tools and headed for the coast. 'Unable to carry the large casks (some of them containing up to 70 gallons of rum), they were breaking them open where they lay, filling any suitable container that came to hand or just consuming large quantities in drunken orgies on the shore.' [Peter C Miller, *Galloway Shipwrecks*].

Logan House, to the north of the village, began as a classical edifice of the early 1700s but was enveloped by an 1874 remodelling in the Scots Baronial style. When Ronald Olaf Hambro (see below) owned it in the 1950s, he had it stripped back to the original, the result of which was described in *Country Life* magazine as 'an architectural miracle'.

Logan Botanic Garden is the most celebrated example in Galloway of the horticultural benefits of the Gulf Stream. Though the McDoualls had long been the lairds of Logan, it was not until the second half of the nineteenth century that the garden started to take off under their ownership. In 1869 James McDouall married Agnes Buchan-Hepburn from Smeaton in East Lothian. It was she who was the keen gardener and she began experimenting with exotic plantings. Her sons, Kenneth and Douglas, carried on her work, travelling the world in search of species that might take to the mild climate of the Rhins. Many years before the garden formally became a tourist attraction, it was reported that 'the proprietor kindly allows visitors to enter the grounds and behold these treasures.'

In his will Kenneth McDouall left the estate to his cousin Sir Ninian Buchan-Hepburn. In 1949 it was sold to the London-based merchant banker Ronald Olaf Hambro. After Hambro's death in 1961, the garden was administered by a trust, but the money ran out and the estate was given to the nation. While the house itself was sold back to Sir Ninian, the by-now famous garden became, and remains, an outpost of the Royal Botanic Garden in Edinburgh. A majority of the plants now on view to the public originated from the Southern Hemisphere. One notable feature of the garden is that it has almost forty species of gum tree.

The village has attracted film directors over the years. Some scenes for *The Wicker Man* were shot here (see Part 2 - The Movies), while in 2000 a BBC drama team began using Port Logan for a series called ***Two Thousand Acres of Sky***. The village was dressed up to look like the fictional island of 'Ronansay' off Skye. When one of the stars of the drama returned to open a fete, Port Logan was reported to have had 'its first ever traffic jam'.

Port Logan Inn

Portpatrick

For well over two hundred years a titanic battle against the elements was waged to try to keep the 'port' in Portpatrick. Even after it had become obvious that the cause was a hopeless one, the investment continued. But, in the end, Portpatrick had to bow to the inevitable and accept that its exposure to the extremes of weather made it ill-suited to be Scotland's principal terminal for sea traffic with Ireland. Portpatrick's loss was Stranraer's gain.

It is not surprising that for so long Portpatrick had seemed to be the ideal **maritime gateway** to and from Ireland, being only some twenty miles from the port of Donaghadee on the other side of the North Channel. The notion of exploiting such a short distance tantalised entrepreneurs and governments for generations. In the early seventeenth century the first to develop the sea link in a concerted way was Sir Hugh Montgomery (1560-1636), an Ayrshire laird who bought the Portree estate, including the harbour, and used it in his role as a leading agent in the Protestant 'plantation' of Catholic Ireland (see Part 2 – The Irish Connection). In 1616 he obtained a royal warrant stipulating that the official route between south-west Scotland and the Ards peninsula would be that between Port Montgomery, as he liked to call it, and Donaghadee in County Down (the latter is recalled in the naming of Portpatrick's Downshire Arms Hotel).

Portpatrick by William Daniell (1816)

Portpatrick continued to benefit from being the British government's first choice for communications with Ireland. An official obsession with its perceived **strategic value** helped to obscure the harbour's fundamental unsuitability. It was via this route that troop deployments were conducted, and for this purpose a military road was laid across Galloway in the 1760s, terminating at Portpatrick. A **new pier** was constructed in the 1770s and in 1790 a regular cross-channel mail service was started.

Before the building of the new pier, sailing in and out of Portpatrick had been a pretty hit-or-miss affair. The engineer John Smeaton described the harbour as being 'almost in a state of nature' and, short though it was, the crossing could be disconcertingly rough (see Part 2 – The Irish Connection). The writer James Boswell's general impression of Portpatrick at this time was not flattering: 'It is a poor town, and instead of appearing a very public thoroughfare as it really is, it looks like a remote Highland seacoast village.'

By the end of the eighteenth century, however, Portpatrick was starting to prosper more conspicuously. The harbour was busy with the import of Irish cattle bound for the markets of England, and the passenger traffic would soon be augmented by the village's rather scandalous status as the 'Gretna Green for Ireland' (see Part 2 – The Irish Connection). Around 1815 the traveller and engraver William Daniell recorded that the place was 'chiefly supported by the constant concourse of passengers by the packets..., almost every house being an inn'. According to Daniell, the briskness of trade had given rise to the Wigtownshire wideboy:

> There is a class of useful persons here whose collective title has never found a place in the list of trades of any guild, livery, or corporation, in the kingdom. They are called the 'Robbery', and ply at the harbour as porters for the service of passengers either landing or embarking. This designation was probably conferred upon them in consequence of their exorbitant charges, and is certainly a humorous but effectual way of warning the public against imposition.

Amidst the prosperity there were nonetheless siren voices warning of the port's vulnerability to the weather and predicting that sooner or later its unsuitability for this major role would become apparent. After a visit in 1802 the engineer Thomas Telford highlighted not only the heavy swell caused by the maelstrom of winds but also the 'large reefs of rock' that made navigation into the harbour hazardous, and he concluded that the location 'was destitute of the advantages requisite for a perfect Harbour for packets to ply from'.

The authorities overlooked Telford's advice and pressed ahead. The engineer John Rennie was hired to design harbour improvements and in 1821 work began on a grand scheme with piers at both the north and south ends. The works required were on a huge scale and went on intermittently for the next fifteen years, employing at times over 700 men. The south pier was finally completed in 1836 but three years later it was destroyed by storms. The idea of adding a north pier was abandoned.

Telford's analysis had been vindicated but the lesson had still not been fully learned. In the 1860s one final push to fulfil Portpatrick's aspiration was undertaken on the back of a government assurance that, if the town were to be connected to the national system of railways, its mail service, which had been suspended, could be re-instated. On this understanding the railway developers, who for the sake of their shareholders should not have ventured beyond Stranraer, decided to lay a track to the western seaboard. Work began on a new harbour basin to accommodate the steamers that were now replacing sailing-ships but, when the Stranraer-Portpatrick section of the railway was opened in 1862, there were no mail boats. There never would be. The preferred option as a mail terminal was now Holyhead in north-west Wales; with faster steamships now in service, there was no longer such a premium on shortness of distance across the water.

The Portpatrick Hotel overlooking the harbour

The harbour had even been given its own dedicated railway halt. This was a white elephant from day one, and, while Portpatrick station itself remained operational until 1951, Portpatrick Harbour station was shut down almost as soon as it was opened up. In 1868 the Irish ferry service was transferred to Stranraer. In the 1870s maintenance of Portpatrick's harbour was discontinued and Nature was allowed to take its devastating course. This was the result by the late nineteenth century, as witnessed by the Galloway travel writer Malcolm Harper:

> The destruction which had been wrought in the solid masonry of the piers was almost incredible. No description could give any idea of the havoc. It must be seen to be believed. The strong iron girders and bolts used in riveting together the ponderous stones forming the breastworks had been in many places snapped asunder like straws, and the great stones tossed about like peas.

Portpatrick developed instead as a leisure and golfing **resort**. The golf course was established in 1903. Two years later the grand hilltop Portpatrick Hotel was completed, and it prospered so well that within a few years it was being extended. According to a contemporary observer, the hotel had all the finest innovations of the time 'with internal furnishings, so extensive and luxurious that, on entering the spacious hall, one has a feeling that the North British Station Hotel has been transported from "Auld Reekie" to this airy home of the gull and the seamew.' A railways-sponsored guidebook of 1910, describing the resort as the 'Elysium of the South-

West', lavished praise on the hotel: 'When it is known that the management has been undertaken by Mr J P Mair, well known in Cairo as having for so many years ably directed the Mena House Hotel, it must be felt that no hotel in the West of Scotland can hope to surpass the new establishment in comfort and sound management'.

Even at Portpatrick's **old parish kirk**, in St Patrick's Street, there are striking reminders of the town's maritime past. The unusual circular tower, thought to be of the sixteenth century, served in the early days as a landmark for seafarers. The adjacent kirk was added in the 1620s at the expense of the port's first developer Sir Hugh Montgomery. The perils of the sea are recalled in the gravestone inscription for William McClean of Ballyclare who was drowned at Carrickfergus in 1831: 'His body having been wafted to the Scottish coast, was found near Portpatrick, and here decently interred by the friendly and generous inhabitants.'

The Kirk's landmark for seafarers

At Black Head to the north-west of Portpatrick, **Killantringan Lighthouse** was the last of those to be built on the Rhins and is another product of the Stevenson lighthouse-building dynasty, this time David A Stevenson, cousin of the writer Robert Louis Stevenson. Killantringan began operating in 1900. It had a fog signal but this was discontinued in 1987, and the light itself was automated the following year. The outbuildings now form a guesthouse.

Of the many **shipwrecks** on the perilous rocks around Portpatrick, the most tragic was that of the paddle-steamer *Orion*. On a June evening in 1850 it was on its way from Liverpool to Glasgow with 160 passengers and 37 crew on board, when it struck the Barnaugh rock and sank within ten minutes. Sixty people died, some of them drowning after an overloaded lifeboat capsized. For

Killantringan Lighthouse

many of the passengers this had been the first stage in their voyage of migration to the New World. One would-be emigrant lost his wife, three daughters and his life-savings of 600 sovereigns, and ended up destitute.

It was incompetence rather than bad weather that caused the shipwreck. The Captain and the 2nd Mate, the latter of whom was at the helm at the time, were tried and found guilty of ‘culpable neglect of duty’. The sum of £200 was raised in Glasgow as a gift for the people of Portpatrick who had done so much to help the survivors.

Southwards along the coast, **Dunskey Castle**, a spectacular ruin looking across the water to Ireland, has the Emerald Isle, appropriately enough, woven into its history. It was the stronghold of the Adairs, a dynasty of Irish origin who distinguished themselves in the murky politics of late-medieval Wigtownshire. An earlier structure was destroyed in the 1490s by their rivals, the McCullochs and the McDoualls. The present fabric dates largely from the middle of the sixteenth century. It was enlarged in the 1620s after Sir Hugh Montgomery (see above) acquired it from the Adairs, who then returned to the country of their forefathers as part of the Protestant plantation then being masterminded by the new laird of Dunskey (see Part 2 – The Irish Connection).

After Montgomery’s death the castle and estate passed into the hands of the Blairs. They soon aspired towards something more commodious, and stone from the castle was used for the building around 1700 of **Dunskey House** on the other side of Portpatrick. The house’s appearance today, however, stems from a complete re-build, in revivalist Scots Baronial style, which was completed in 1904.

In the late eighteenth century the Blairs became the Hunter-Blairs when Jane Blair of Dunskey inherited her father's estate and her husband, James Hunter, added her surname to his. As businessman and banker, **Sir James Hunter-Blair** (1741-1787) had parallel lives: one around Portpatrick, where he was actively involved in the harbour developments; the other in Edinburgh, whose MP he was for four years and whose Lord Provost he became in 1784. He befriended Robert Burns when the poet visited the capital in 1786 following the triumphant publication of his Kilmarnock edition. Within months, at the age of forty-six, Hunter-Blair was dead and Burns wrote an elegy for him in which Mother Caledonia appears during a storm to mourn her loss:

'My Patriot falls – but shall he lie unsung,
  While empty Greatness saves a worthless name?
No: every Muse shall join her tuneful tongue,
  And future ages hear his growing fame.

'And I will join a Mother's tender cares,
  Thro' future times to make his virtues last,
That distant years may boast of other BLAIRS – '
  She said, and vanish'd with the sweeping blast.

Hunter-Blair lives on in other ways. Edinburgh's Hunter Square and Blair Street are named after him, as is (one presumes) Portpatrick's Blair Terrace.

Dunskey Castle

Port William

There had long been a settlement here where the Killantrae Burn enters the east side of Luce Bay. The fishing was good and the burn provided power for mills. But the biggest component of its early economy was **smuggling** via the Isle of Man. In the second half of the eighteenth century the contraband trade was so substantial here that in 1788 a military barracks and a customs post were established. Many of the surrounding farmhouses had 'brandy-holes' for the concealment of illicit goods. The most notorious was Clone Farm, about which Sir Herbert Maxwell wrote in his *History of Dumfries and Galloway* (1896) with a personal slant:

> In the year 1894, the author had to lay out money in reconstructing a barn at the farm of Clone, the floor of which had given way and fallen into an old 'brandy-hole' underneath. At this farm there was formerly a concealed store-cellar of a very ingenious kind. Two subterranean chambers were constructed, one under the other. The excisemen were freely admitted to the upper one, and, not unnaturally, never thought of searching beneath it. But in the lower one, which was approached by a separate subterranean entrance, good store of contraband material was constantly kept.

From the 1770s onwards Sir Herbert's ancestor, Sir William Maxwell of Monreith, started developing the village and of course named it after himself. A proper **harbour** was built in the 1790s,

Port William harbour at low tide

with later expansion and improvement, and it became the principal port serving the western Machars. Trading with Ireland was fairly common and, according to a local information board, this had interesting horticultural repercussions: 'Many of the village gardens have rich dark soil which was carried as ballast and left here if the schooner arrived to collect a cargo.' There was a certain amount of ship-building too. A sloop of 1818, owned by Sir William himself, was cheekily named after the Walter Scott smuggling character *Dirk Hatteraick*.

The arrival of the Wigtownshire railway in the 1870s did not entirely kill off Port William's maritime business. In the early years of the twentieth century it could still be described as 'a place of some importance, with a branch Bank, several good shops, and a harbour with a considerable coasting trade'. Heavy goods continued to be delivered by sea until the 1930s.

The flat-capped man leaning on a fence and staring out to sea is able to remain absolutely motionless because he is a **sculpture**. Andrew Brown's original version in concrete deteriorated, so the community raised funds to have it re-done in bronze.

The author makes a friend

On the coast to the north-west of the village the naming of **Philip and Mary Point** is a conundrum. It is said that in 1588 a vessel of the Spanish Armada came aground here. The defeated fleet, having taken a long homeward escape route round the north of Scotland, back down the west coast and along the Atlantic fringe of Ireland, lost a lot of ships on the journey. Although the route taken was nowhere near the Solway, it is possible that a damaged vessel drifted into Luce Bay. The problem with the story is that there is no official record of the alleged incident and no ship of this name appears on the list of Armada vessels unaccounted for. The only source for the tale is the Agnew family. Sir Andrew, in his history of the Agnews as hereditary sheriffs, claims that his ancestor Sir Patrick saw not only the wreck in question but also two others along the Wigtownshire coastline, one at Money Head north-west of Port Logan, the other on the shore by Cruggleton Castle south of Garlieston.

In the case of 'Philip and Mary' it tends to be assumed that the name comes from that of a ship (actual or imaginary). This is puzzling. Yes, the aggressor Philip of Spain had indeed been married to a Mary – Mary of England. But when the Armada set off, that Mary had already been dead for thirty years. Would a foreign fleet aiming at the conquest of England really have included a vessel named partly after a former queen of the enemy? Or perhaps the Mary is Mary Queen of Scots who fondly imagined that her fellow Catholic monarch Philip would one day come and rescue her from her English incarceration. After all this time and in the absence of any authorities other than a single amateur historian of the nineteenth century, we shall probably never know the truth.

The remains of Chapel Finian on the shore of Luce Bay

Further along the coast to the north-west **Chapel Finian** is of the tenth or eleventh century and dedicated to the Irish saint Finian, who is said to have studied at Whithorn and to have influenced St Columba of Iona. The chapel may have been used by Whithorn-bound pilgrims arriving by sea.

At Drumtroddan farm, to the north-east, are constructions of a markedly different vintage: a trio of **standing stones** from possibly the second millennium BC. Well, two of them are still standing; the middle one has fallen over. 'Set on a SE-facing slope, this row is thought to have been aligned on the SW midwinter sunset,' according to a Scottish archaeological guide by Anna and Graham Ritchie.

Drumtroddan farm also has **cup-and-ring markings** (see Part 2 – The Early History).

Drumtroddan standing stones and cup-and-ring carvings

Sandhead

The north-west shore of Luce Bay is known as Luce Sands and Sandhead no doubt took its name from that. However, judging from the settlement's position in relation to the sands, a more accurate name would surely have been Sandbottom. The proliferation of caravanning and camping facilities testifies to the popularity of this stretch of the shore as a place of relaxation. The industrial bustle of Sandhead Creamery is now gone, the building turned into a block of flats.

Long before its rather unexciting English name came into usage, the area was known as Balgreggan [Gaelic *baile a' ghragain*, 'fermtoun of the manor']. To the north of the village, **Balgreggan motte** is where Norman immigrants of the twelfth or thirteenth century would have had a castle. Archaeological evidence suggests it was of timber and that at some point it was burnt down. Many centuries later the motte was used as an observation post during the Second World War. To the west of the motte there was the grand Balgreggan House, designed by William Adam and built around 1730. It was demolished in the mid-1960s.

The **'Balgreggan Hoard'** is the term given to a collection of Roman coins found at a quarry here in 1913. The discovery does not

indicate a settled Roman presence. The imperialists did not show a great deal of interest in the northern Solway region much further west than the Fleet valley in Kirkcudbrightshire. The coins demonstrate that the native tribes around Luce Bay did rather well out of selling supplies to the nearby occupiers.

South-west of Sandhead, **Kirkmadrine** is a holy site of such antiquity that memorial stones found here are among the very earliest Christian remains in Scotland. Only the 'Latinus' stone at the Whithorn Priory Museum is older.

The Kirkmadrine stones range in time from the Dark Ages to the medieval period. But three of them, all from the fifth century, attract special attention. They are decorated with the *Chi-Rho*, the Christian monogram made from the first two letters in the Greek version of 'Christ', a symbol introduced by the Roman emperor Constantine when he converted to Christianity in the fourth century. Two of the stones commemorate priests with Latinised names like Viventius, Mavorius and Florentius. The third stone has a Latin inscription INITIUM ET FINIS - 'the beginning and the end', an echo of Revelation from the New Testament. According to Daphne Brooke in *Wild Men and Holy Places* (1994), these and the stones of the same period from Whithorn indicate a prolonged contact between Galloway and a Christian centre in western Gaul: 'The formulae of these inscriptions closely resemble those of classical paganism, and so mark them as very early Christian; but the wording is distinctive and manifestly Christian in content. With one exception [in Wales], nothing similar is known in Britain; but counterparts are to be found between the river Loire and the Pyrenees and especially around Poitiers.'

Kirkmadrine's most precious trio of memorials went missing for many years. The story of what happened to them and of how they were found again has an almost farcical aspect. Our modern reverence for heritage was not shared by our forebears, who saw in things of the past only potential for re-cycling in the present. In Kirkmadrine's case, in the mid-1800s fifth-century holy artefacts were converted, in a glorious show of indifference, into gate-posts.

In 1861 the archaeologist Arthur Mitchell visited Kirkmadrine and came across the two taller stones in a most unexpected way:

> When climbing over the gate, I observed that there was a figure and an inscription on the stone pillar on which it was hung. The figure I recognised as one which I had seen in the Catacombs at Rome, and the inscription, which was easily read, appeared to me of remarkable interest. I knew enough of our sculptured stones to be immediately aware that I had fallen on something which had no counterpart anywhere else in Scotland…I found that the other pillar, to which the gate fell, had a similar figure on it, and also what appeared to be a continuation of the inscription.

Mitchell inquired among the local farmers and found general awareness of there having been a third stone, but no one knew its whereabouts. He met a retired schoolmaster, William Todd, who forty years earlier had sketched in minute detail all three stones when they were still in their original positions – documentary evidence that would later prove crucial in identification. This third stone, which came to be known as 'the missing stone of Kirkmadrine', took on the aura of a kind of archaeologist's Holy Grail, but it remained maddeningly elusive.

Meanwhile, in 1877, the Rev George Phillip had become minister at the Free Kirk in Sandhead. He too was of an antiquarian bent, knew of the missing stone, and tried hard to find it. But his efforts were also in vain. Then one day in 1916 a Sandhead stonemason, Robert Nelson, interrupted his repairing of the manse gate to come to the minister's door with a grave announcement. 'Excuse me, Sir, will ye come oot to the gate. I've broken the lost stone of Kirkmadrine.'

It was only after smashing a hefty stone into smaller bits for the better re-building of the gate-pier that Nelson had noticed the carvings. Many years later the minister's nephew, Professor

Charles McNeil, recounted the scene on that day:

> Two elderly men standing bare-headed by the gate; and at their feet an ancient famous stone, a stone of destiny, in shattered fragments. Each man was deeply concerned with this broken block of whinstone. The minister had searched for it during forty years and had passed it close by every day as he went through his gate. The mason had found it by lucky chance and then had smashed it with his hammer. So do the fates play their tricks on mortal men.

The fragments were cemented together so successfully that the joints are practically invisible, and today the stone that almost met its *finis* has a fresh *initium* alongside its fifth-century companions in the special glass-fronted display porch at the west end of Kirkmadrine kirk.

Until being united with Stoneykirk, Kirkmadrine was a parish in its own right under the name of Toskerton. The site may well have had an early monastery associated with Whithorn. Later there was a medieval kirk, which was abandoned and fell into ruins. The present building is not so much a kirk as a mausoleum chapel, built in the late nineteenth century for Lady McTaggart Stewart of Ardwell. Its design, revivalist Romanesque, was based on Cruggleton Kirk.

Kirkmadrine

Sorbie

The village once had a national reputation for the quality of its **damask weaving**. The cloth was made from locally-grown flax. The industry, employing at its height some ninety people, operated between about 1790 and 1850. In 1834 Sorbie damask won a prize for the best of its type in Scotland. The 7th Earl of Galloway developed the village to accommodate the weavers.

Many of the earls are buried in their family vault at the former, and now ruinous, **parish kirk**, which had been replaced in the 1870s by a new kirk towards the east and closer to Garlieston. Until 1950 Sorbie had a **railway station** and until 1991 an adjacent **creamery**.

The farm of Balsier to the south of Sorbie was the birthplace, in 1750, of the physician and highly eccentric man of letters **Robert Couper** (see Part 2 – The Writers).

The Sorbie **way of life**, as it was until relatively recently and certainly still within living memory, is charmingly described in *The Third Statistical Account of Scotland*, most of whose parish appraisals for the Shire were written around 1950 though the book was not published until 1965. It seems now like something from an age of innocence:

Of juvenile delinquency there is none...The community is law-abiding apart from occasional quarrels among men under the influence of drink. The parish presents an appearance of well-being and prosperity, for there are no ragged persons and the children are well and tastefully dressed...It is true that some of the older retired people conceal straitened circumstances under an appearance of tidiness, cleanliness and cheerfulness; a few of the aged live alone and need a helping neighbourly hand, which is always forthcoming, but they resent any suggestion of a move to a relative or to a home.

The area around here is the land of the **Hannays** (though some of them branched off to Kirkdale across Wigtown Bay in Kirkcudbrightshire). 'Hannay' covers a multitude of spellings including Hanna, Hannah and Hanney; while, further back in time, they pop up in the records variously as A'Hannay, A'hanna, Ahannay, de Hannethe and de Annethe. They were, in the fashion of the times, belligerent and engaged in running feuds with their neighbours, the Dunbars, the Murrays, the Stewarts and the Kennedys.

Sorbie Tower

Their stronghold **Sorbie Tower** or Old Place of Sorbie, to the east of the village, was built in the late sixteenth century. But the site had been developed for many centuries before that. The evidence of that lies a short distance to the south-west of the tower: the twelfth-century man-made **motte** on which there would have been a small timber castle within a protective wall or palisade. Waterlogged surroundings added substantially to the site's defensibility (the name Sorbie derives from Norse and means 'swamp farm'). It is likely that this earlier construction was for the Veteriponte (or Vieuxpont) family, Anglo-Norman incomers who were related through marriage to Roland, Lord of Galloway. The Hannays did not take over the Sorbie estate until the fifteenth century, though they had been long established elsewhere in Wigtownshire.

Sorbie Tower was occupied until 1748. Its final resident was John Stewart, who became MP for Wigtownshire in the new Union parliament of 1707. The building fell into such a ruinous state that by the 1950s it was dangerous to visit. Then the worldwide Hannay diaspora, including an Australian cartoonist/impresario, came to the rescue. In 1960 the Clan Hannay Society was formed 'with the hope that one day the ancestral home of the family in Scotland would be acquired'. It was indeed acquired in 1965 and measures were taken to halt the tower's further deterioration.

The Hannays having largely disappeared from Sorbie, the Kirkcudbrightshire branch at Kirkdale assumed leadership of this latter-day clan. Its first declared 'chief' was Major Ramsay Rainsford Hannay. When he died in 2004 at the age of ninety-three, he was succeeded by his son Professor David Hannay. Offices of the society include 'Constable of Sorbie Tower' and 'Keeper of the Tartan'.

The early-seventeenth-century poet **Patrick Hannay** (died around 1630) is believed to have had a Sorbie connection, though his exact parentage has never been established. He appears to have flourished in or around the London court of James VI after the Scottish king inherited the crown of England in 1603. His published works included a couple of elegies on the death in 1619 of James's wife, Anne of Denmark.

Though a practitioner of the peaceful art of verse, the poet was not entirely devoid of the fighting spirit of the Hannays. He joined a volunteer force that set sail from Leith in 1620 at the start of the continental Thirty Years' War. They were rushing to the defence of King James's daughter Elizabeth, wife of Frederick, Elector of the Palatinate [south-west Germany]. The trouble had been started by the Elector and Elizabeth's accepting the crown of Bohemia, a Protestant move to which the countries of the Catholic League responded with an overwhelming show of force. The plucky efforts of Hannay and his fellow warriors were fruitless: Frederick and Elizabeth (the 'Winter Queen') not only were ousted from Bohemia but also lost their original Palatinate.

Stairhaven

The early-twentieth-century Galloway guide-book author C H Dick gave four reasons for wanting to visit this out-of-the-way seaside place: 'I liked its name, George Borrow [the writer] visited it, it has a practically disused harbour, and it was once a haunt of smugglers.' It used to be known as the Crow's Nest until the Earl of Stair developed it into a wee **port** in the 1840s and renamed it after himself. Dick thought the pier a 'gigantic structure for so small a port' and wrote of the place's 'curious sense of desolation in its apparent abandonment'.

Apart from when it thrived as a smuggling 'haven' in the late eighteenth century, no visitor seems to have ever found it anything but inactive. George Borrow, after visiting in July 1866, noted in his journal: 'a house by the sea side; little pier; a few fishing boats; place seemingly deserted.' Incidentally, Borrow, on his way to Stairhaven from his lodgings in Glenluce, took a dip in Luce Bay and afterwards recorded: 'some people bathing; none could swim; seemed surprised that I could'.

On the shore south of Stairhaven there is the site of a prehistoric **broch** (there is another at Ardwell Point – see Ardwell for background on brochs).

To the south-east are the remains of **Sinniness Castle**, a Kennedy tower-house of the late sixteenth century. Now, 'Sinniness'...there's a formidable word! According to the ever-wise John MacQueen (*Place-Names in the Rhinns of Galloway and Luce Valley*), its origin is Scandanavian (remember the Norsemen/Vikings came here): a compound of *sin*, 'bladder serge' and *nes*, 'promontory, headland'. Sinniness Castle means, therefore, 'castle of the promontory on which bladder serge grows'!

Stoneykirk

Is 'stoney' quite what it seems? Place-name specialists cannot agree on the derivation. One theory is that the origin lies in the Scandanavian occupation of the area in the ninth and tenth centuries. So it could be from Norse *steinna akr*, 'field of stones'. But in *The Place-Names of Galloway* Sir Herbert Maxwell is adamant that it 'has nothing to do with stones.' He goes with the alternative explanation that the medieval kirk was dedicated to St Stephen and that 'Stephen's Kirk' evolved in Scots to 'Steeniekirk' and later 'Stainiekirk'. Maxwell asserts that this in turn 'was interpreted as "stoney" by English clerks and map-makers'.

The **kirk** building that can be seen today dates from 1827. It has been out of ecclesiastical use since 1988.

Stoneykirk is said to have been the scene of a sacrilegious **murder** around 1700. According to the story, the Rev Robert Campbell, who became the minister in 1697, was bumped off in a dispute between the MacDoualls of Balgreggan and the MacDoualls of Garthland over which family was more directly descended from the Lords of Galloway. Campbell tended to favour the Garthland claim, thus incurring the wrath of the Balgreggan bunch. For fear of being poisoned by the disgruntled party, the minister took the precaution of never accepting food or drink when calling upon them. He was finally eliminated, however, through the treachery of the Balgreggan housekeeper. Pretending to be seeking spiritual guidance, she invited the minister into her quarters and persuaded him to have a glass of wine. 'It is said', according to one account, ‘that when he crossed the Sand Bill Burn his body was already swelling, and that before he reached a farm half a mile farther on the buttons were bursting off his waistcoat’.

Proximity to the shore of Luce Bay meant that from the late eighteenth century onwards the gathering and burning of **kelp** or seaweed provided seasonal employment for the Stoneykirk area. The ash had an application in various chemical processes. It was particularly useful in the processing of cloth. In the 1790s it was recorded that there were four flax mills and a bleachfield in the parish. Though all traces of this industry have disappeared, there are still remains to the south-east of the village of a seventeenth-century **windmill**.

Stranraer

From the earliest times Stranraer had all the natural factors favouring the creation of a settlement. There were good sources of water from a burn and from a well; within Loch Ryan there was shelter from the high seas (the town's motto is *Tutissima Statio*, 'safest harbour'); and there was an excellent supply of food from the plentiful fish of the loch.

It was already a significant centre of power for the original Brittonic people when the Romans arrived in the first century AD and named them the Novantae. Using the information that the Roman surveyors had gathered in their first foray into the territory the second-century cartographer Ptolemy identified on his famous world map a place along the shores of the loch which he called **Rerigonium**, 'very royal place'. The map was not entirely accurate and the precise location of this original settlement has never been satisfactorily established. But 'Ryan' undoubtedly relates to 'Rerigonium'.

Stranraer was formally created in 1595 when the powerful Adair family were successful in having it turned into a **burgh of barony**, much to the consternation at the time of the burgh of Wigtown, which felt that its own exclusive trading rights were being undermined. In 1617 King James VI and I raised Stranraer's status to that of a **royal burgh**.

But the town remained for a long time a loose confederation of separate small settlements. The burn (now hidden beneath North Strand Street) was an important dividing-line. On the west side was the embryonic '**Stronrawyr**'. On the east side was a community known as **Chapel**, named after an Adair religious foundation dedicated to St John. It was here also that a castle was built, which to this day is known as the Castle of St John (see below). Nearby there were also the clachans of **Clayhole** and **Hillhead**. All eventually coalesced into modern Stranraer but the distinct identities were jealously maintained for a long time to come. Perhaps to promote a greater sense of unity, one of the rules of the early burgh was that all house-holders should attend any funeral (though if the deceased was 'of mein estait', then sending along a servant as proxy would suffice!). Even as late as the 1870s inhabitants of Clayhole and Hillhead were objecting to having to pay Stranraer's local taxes. The slow, piecemeal pace of municipal merger may well help to explain the irregularity of the street pattern, which is still evident to this day.

There is some debate about the origin of the 'Stranraer' **place-name**. The popular theory used to be that it meant a 'rawer' or row of houses along a 'strand' (note today's North Strand Street and South Strand Street). That interpretation never seemed very convincing and learned opinion now inclines towards a rather complicated derivation from Irish/Scottish Gaelic words meaning either 'big stream' (ie a reference to the central burn) or 'stream swarming with herring'.

The **Castle of St John**, an imposing sight in the centre of the modern town, is Stranraer's oldest building. It was built for Ninian Adair of Kinhilt around 1510 and re-modelled around 1600. During the 'Killing Time' of the 1680s it was the headquarters of the government troops while they conducted their ferocious crackdown on the hardline Presbyterians of the Covenanter movement. In the 1820s part of the building was converted into a prison, the roof being adapted as an exercise yard. In 1990 the castle was opened to the public as an historic visitor attraction.

Though Stranraer would eventually supersede the older Wigtown as the county's commercial capital, prosperity was slow to come. The cost of bringing fuel to the town was frequently blamed for the lack of growth in manufacturing. In 1656 it was reported that 'there is not now nor ever was any trade to be heard of here'. Half a century later the town was said to be in such a 'low and decayed state' that Scotland's Convention of Royal Burghs granted £40 for the repair of its tolbooth. Towards the end of the eighteenth century the fashion among the rural gentry for having a town house provided one form of economic stimulus, and by the 1770s there were sufficient civic funds for the erection of a handsome town hall, the building in George Street known today as the **Old Town Hall** (now the Stranraer Museum). Despite the growing sophistication of the town, Robert Heron could still describe Stranraer in his 1790s appraisal of Scotland as 'admirably well situated for commerce, yet almost without trade'.

The town authorities began to appreciate that something had to be done about the **harbour**, or rather the lack of one worthy of the term. The town's natural advantages as a maritime haven were not being fully exploited. For too long Stranraer's sea-going trade, which included ship-building and the handling of Baltic timber imports, had been conducted without the convenience of a proper quayside, shipped goods having to be transferred onto smaller vessels for onshore delivery. At last in the 1820s a quayside was constructed. This was what is now known as the **West Pier**.

It was the next phase of infrastructure improvement that transformed Stranraer into the marine gateway to Ireland as we know it today. In 1861 the extension to the town of the **railway** system became operational. There were two stations, one for the town-centre, the other for the harbour. The aim of the latter was to link up with a ferry service to Ireland, and for this purpose the **East Pier** was built at the same time. Within a few years Stranraer had entirely replaced Portpatrick as the main terminal for the North Channel and, in 1872, the first timetabled service to Larne in Northern Ireland was inaugurated by the paddle-steamer *Princess Louise*. The town had finally found a sure source of prosperity. As if in celebration of renewed civic self-confidence, the **New Town Hall** (and sheriff court) in Lewis Street was opened in 1874.

Stranraer 'New' Town Hall and Sheriff Court

Stranraer has continued to respond to the needs of the ferry operators. The East Pier was substantially extended in the 1890s and a new railway station built. In the 1970s the station was rebuilt and an extra pier created to accommodate larger vessels. Though the 'Paddy' line from Dumfries in the east closed in the mid-1960s, rail passengers continue to arrive at the harbour station from Glasgow and Ayrshire in the north. As they progress up Loch Ryan, they might like to compare their own impressions with those recorded in the 1930s by the novelist Freeman Wills Crofts (see Part 2 – Other Pairs of Eyes).

The *Princess Victoria* memorial

In Agnew Park next to the West Pier, the ***Princess Victoria*** **Memorial** is a poignant reminder of the potential perils of even a short sea-crossing. In January 1953 the Larne-bound car ferry sank in the North Channel with the loss of 133 lives (see Part 2 – The Irish Connection).

With the continuous need for dredging and the lack of room for further expansion at Stranraer harbour, the town's future as a ferry base has been much discussed over recent years. At the time of writing, a plan for a total relocation to Cairnryan has been put into abeyance. But one day the blueprint may come back off the shelf. In anticipation of major change, the town is now re-positioning itself increasingly towards servicing the **leisure and tourism** industries.

Boats and betting seem to be the two key elements. The area lends itself perfectly to the development of a recreational marina. More controversial has been the town's application for the right to operate a casino. In 2008 the British government announced that Stranraer would be the only place in Scotland to be granted a casino licence. A Dumfries and Galloway Council spokesman stated: 'The plans are not just about a casino. It's about the re-

Agnew Park on Stranraer's waterfront

generation of the Stranraer/Loch Ryan waterfront and the transformation from port town to high-quality marine leisure destination'. A less sanguine commentary came in a terse letter to a national newspaper: 'So Gordon Brown's answer to the problems that Stranraer has with drugs and alcohol is – give it a casino too. Maybe he hopes the addicts will spend their money on the 80 one-arm bandits instead'.

Proximity to Ireland has had a profound impact on the history of Stranraer, as it has on that of the whole county, and not least on the character of local speech. The steady trickle of Irish migration that began in the middle of the eighteenth century had, by the middle of the following century, swelled to such a torrent that it was publicly debated as a major social problem. *The Statistical Account* of 1839 reported: 'Of late years a great many of the natives of the sister island, having left their country in quest of food and employment, have located themselves in hovels erected in the lanes and outskirts of the town, and depend, in great measure, for subsistence, on the charity of the inhabitants.' Owing to the density of the Irish population, an area to the south of the town-centre came to be known as **Little Ireland**, and it included Little Dublin Street (see Part 2 – The Irish Connection).

At one time Stranraer was the base for a substantial local **fishing** industry. The herring, which were once abundant, eventually disappeared from Loch Ryan, except that from time to time they would come back again, as this early-twentieth-century observer noted:

> Recently...they have shown signs of returning – perhaps owing to systematic persecution in other haunts. In 1907, they came into the loch in shoals, and 50 boats might be seen at one time, busily plying their nets for weeks together. As many as three million herrings are said to have been landed on the quay at Stranraer in one day.

Oysters were also once more abundant in Loch Ryan than they are now. Yields were at their highest in 1910, when a fleet of thirty boats landed some 130 tonnes of them. That level of production lasted for a decade or so, after which the fishery fell away to such an extent that by the late 1950s the industry was finished. However, after scientific monitoring of the beds, the fishery eventually revived and today, though the catches are a small fraction of peak rates, it is still the largest native oyster fishery in Scotland.

Close to the ferry terminal, the original part of the **North West Castle**, now expanded into a hotel, was built in the 1820s as the home of the Arctic explorer Sir John Ross, and was so named in recognition of his valiant attempts to navigate the North West Passage (see Part 2 – Celebrities of the Shire). Nautical features were incorporated into the design of the house (a 'castle' only in name). In the early twentieth century, when it was still a private house, a visitor described its dining-room annexe: 'In designing it Sir John took a ship's cabin as his model. The room is lighted only from above, the wall at one end is curved as in a ship's stern, and a continuous row of mirrors runs along one side. The denial of a view outwards is rather oppressive; but this, with the subdued light, only helps the intended effect.'

The North West Castle became a hotel in 1962 and has grown in size from twelve bedrooms to more than eighty. In 1970 it acquired the first-ever indoor curling rink. The ice would have brought back vivid memories for Sir John.

The North West Castle Hotel

Stranraer Football Club is Wigtownshire's only team participating in Scotland's professional league structure. Although the club was formed as far back as 1870, the 'Blues' had a long struggle to get senior status, allegedly because the football authorities were prejudiced against the town owing to its peripheral location. Finally in 1955 they were elected to the then Scottish B division. A new main stand was built in 1995 and now Stair Park has an official capacity of 6000. Given the club's statistical record, its hardcore fan-base is a supreme example of stoicism.

Whauphill

Such a bonnie name! 'Whaup' is Scots for 'curlew'. Hill of the curlews!

Whauphill Village Hall

It requires a flight of the imagination to recall that this now quiet clachan was once connected to the **railway** network. When the Wigtownshire Railway down the Machars from Newton Stewart to Whithorn was built, Whauphill got its very own station. It was opened in 1876 and closed in 1950.

Whauphill has long been associated with the lairds of **Barnbarroch**, the estate lying to the north of the village. The Vaus family first appeared on the scene in the fourteenth century, their surname indicating that their ancestors had been Norman immigrants. By the sixteenth century the name had evolved into Vans, after which it was doubled into Vans Agnew through marriage into a branch of the Agnew dynasty in the early eighteenth century. The Vans Agnews were now so advanced into Galloway society that the building of a mansion at Barnbarroch was called for. The house was completed in 1780 and expanded in the following century. In 1941 it was destroyed by fire after an elderly Vans Agnew female left on a candle which ignited a curtain. The lady died in the blaze. A grand Vans Agnew mausoleum of the eighteenth century is still evident, though damaged, in the kirkyard at Kirkinner.

Barnbarroch House

The most renowned of the Vaus/Vans/Vans Agnew dynasty was **Sir Patrick Vaus** (died 1597), an aide to King James VI. He was part of the deputation sent in 1587 to negotiate James's marriage to Anne of Denmark. When the marriage (or rather the formalisation of an earlier union by proxy) finally took place at Oslo in November 1589, Vaus was there to witness it. The royal contingent stayed on for an extraordinarily self-indulgent Scandanavian holiday over the following five months. The Scots cleric who had performed the ceremony reported that 'Our King [and doubtless Vaus and the other courtiers] made good cheer and drank stoutly till the spring time.'

When Vaus was appointed a judge, he was given the title Lord Barnbarroch.

Due south, agricultural improvement work in the 1860s provided a rare opportunity to study at first hand several **crannogs**, prehistoric loch-dwellings built on wooden piles. The local landowner Sir William Maxwell had had Dowalton Loch drained with the intention of releasing extra farmland but, because of the rocky terrain at the bottom of the loch, his plan was unsuccessful. Victorian archaeologists were thrilled, though. The effect of the draining was that the ancient structures were thoroughly exposed and available for detailed investigation.

Whithorn

Pilgrim procession through Whithorn 1936

Historically, the most significant place in Wigtownshire. This is where the new religion of Christianity first penetrated Scotland and it is often referred to as the **'cradle of Christianity'**. A missionary community was established here by the early 400s, a generation before Columba's mission began on Iona. The dating of the Christian carvings now housed at the Whithorn Priory Museum (see below) is tangible evidence of all of this.

Tradition asserts that Whithorn's first bishop was **Ninian** and that he built a chapel known as the Candida Casa [Latin, 'shining-bright house'], so called because its exotic stone and lime construction was in marked contrast to the dark mud and turf buildings of the native population. There is now much scholarly debate about who exactly Ninian was, if indeed he ever existed, and about when he operated. Nonetheless, a personality accepted as Ninian was later canonised by the Roman Catholic Church, a cult grew around his name and supposed achievements, and right through the Dark and Middle Ages until the sixteenth-century Protestant takeover of Scotland, pilgrims - ranging from kings to commoners - came here to pay their respects and seek cures for their ills. For many centuries the pilgrimage trade was the mainstay of Whithorn's economy. Today's dependence on tourism is nothing new.

The most prestigious of the regular visitors to Whithorn during the later Middle Ages was **King James IV**, who reigned from 1488 to 1513. His first Ninian pilgrimage was 1491 and he re-

The Pend - leading to Whithorn Priory and Parish Kirk

turned often. He would usually arrive with a great entourage, including musicians, and the whole event was turned into a jolly outing. During a stopover at Glenluce Abbey he is said to have lost money betting on games of skittles. His journeys southwards were also excellent opportunities for calling in on one of his numerous mistresses. The king had much need of prayer for forgiveness, not least on account of his own part in the downfall of his father at the hands of court rebels. Though fond of the pleasures of the flesh, he also believed in making himself suffer on the grounds that this might help towards spiritual cleansing. On one pilgrimage he insisted on walking all the way to Whithorn, a journey that took him eight days and required a visit to the shoemaker at Penpont in Dumfriesshire.

When the Christians arrived the indigenous people were the original Brittonic Celts whose society had survived the Roman occupation of southern Scotland. Successive waves of immigration followed: the Anglians of the kingdom of Northumbria, the Irish, the Vikings and eventually the Scots. The Anglians, who ruled for a couple of centuries from about 700, translated 'candida casa' straight into their own language, an early form of English: *hwit earn*, which became modern 'Whithorn'. Throughout all the changes Whithorn still remained an important Christian centre, revolving increasingly around the Ninian cult.

The inward flow of peoples led to continuous building and rebuilding upon the site of the Candida Casa. Excavation work begun in 1984 has revealed some of these earlier foundations. But basically what we see in Whithorn's religious buildings around

Bruce Street today begins with the twelfth century. That was when the cathedral, whose ruins (nave and crypt) are close to the present parish kirk, was begun, under the patronage – it is thought – of Fergus, Lord of Galloway. This edifice was partly re-built in the following century, and enlarged again in the fifteenth century.

Much of the cathedral was lost after the Protestant Reformation. Like most abandoned structures in days gone by, the stonework was taken away for house-building. The cathedral was saved from complete ruination by the nave being converted around 1600 into the parish kirk. Abandonment was total, however, in 1822 when the present parish kirk was completed. It was only towards the end of the nineteenth century that the urge to consolidate these medieval remains was put into action. The 3rd Marquess of Bute, a medievalist with a mania for restoration in Wigtownshire (see Mochrum and Garlieston) and elsewhere, sponsored the work.

Across the road from the Whithorn Priory, the exterior of 76 George Street has a plaque memorialising the **'Galloway Poetess'**. Don't get over-excited by this: in Part 2 – The Writers, you will discover more about the deadly dull doggerel of Jeanie Donnan.

The town of Whithorn had long been a trading burgh under the supervision of the priory but in 1511 became a **Royal Burgh** in its own right. The town's layout is ancient, but the principal buildings lining its streets today are substantially of the nineteenth century. The **Town House** on George Street was completed in 1814. Civic functions were later transferred to the **New Town Hall**, an 1880s building on St John Street, part of the main road leading northwards out of the town. Also in St John Street it is interesting to note, in a town of such antique holiness, that the former United Presbyterian Church now serves as a filling-station.

A new take on the 'parish pump'

Whithorn Priory Museum houses
Scotland's oldest Christian carved stones

The **Whithorn Priory Museum** is home to the Historic Scotland collection of early Christian stone carvings, most of them associated with the 'Whithorn School' of 800-1100 AD but also including highly significant artefacts from previous periods.

The single most important piece is the memorial known as the Latinus Stone. This is the earliest extant Christian stone carving in Scotland. It has been dated to 450 AD. The stone commemorates 35-year-old Latinus and his 4-year-old daughter. 'We praise you, the Lord', the inscription [translated from the Latin] declares. The man's Latin name demonstrates that the Roman Empire continued to exert cultural influence upon the Solway area.

Another cultural influence is apparent in a small number of stones from the 700s. Some of these carry Anglo-Saxon runes, indicative of a powerful Anglian presence in the area during its occupation by the kingdom of Northumbria between about 700 and 900 AD.

The 'Whithorn School' sculptors used mainly local whinstone. They were well aware of how easily this stone split, so they kept their decorative patterns relatively simple and did not carve too deeply into the material. In terms of material, one notable exception is the carving known as the Monreith Cross (because it may have come from Kirkmaiden-in-Fernis near Monreith and stood for years in the garden of Monreith House). This one was done in sandstone, an imported stone.

The **Whithorn Story Visitor Centre** explains not just the 'story' but also how it has been gradually unfolded by more than one hundred years of archaeological investigation. A fascinating range of objects that have been dug up are now on display: the crozier and rings used by a twelfth-century bishop, imported glass and pottery, combs made from antlers. If you ever doubted that the Angles of Northumbria came here, a collection of their coins is

Part of the 'Whithorn Story'

here as incontrovertible proof. Perhaps the most intriguing part of the exhibition is a kind of medieval Lost Property: the personal belongings left behind by many generations of pilgrims.

South-west of Whithorn, **St Ninian's Cave** at Physgill on Luce Bay is said to be where Ninian retreated periodically for contemplation. According to an eighth-century monk, the saint 'studied heavenly wisdom with a devoted mind in a cave of horrible blackness' [translation from Latin]. Because of the tradition it was a must-see attraction for the medieval pilgrims, and they left their mark, Christian graffiti incised into the cave walls. Other, moveable stone carvings with Christian symbolism were taken away for safekeeping in Whithorn following excavations towards the end of the nineteenth century. The Roman Catholic church still holds an annual pilgrimage to this spot.

St Ninian's Cave

To the north-west of Whithorn, the **Swallow Theatre** at Ravenstone is possibly Scotland's most intimate wee venue. Jill and David Sumner bought Moss Park in 1990 because they realised that the outbuildings might give them the opportunity to fulfil their dream of running their own theatre. At first, conversion of the old barn was informal but, after the granting of planning permission, building work began in earnest. The auditorium now has seating for fifty. The stage lighting is powered by solar panels and a wind turbine. The theatre was named after the barn's swallows. 'In the summer, if the weather is fine, we put on productions in the garden, often attended by curious young heifers in the next field!'

There has been disarray over the years in the dating and identification of the great prehistoric earthwork known as **Rispain Camp**, which lies to the south-west of the town. An investigator for the Royal Commission on the Ancient and Historical Monuments of Scotland commented that it was 'an object-lesson in the perils of archaeological field survey and excavation.' At first it was thought to be Roman. Then it was re-classified as a medieval motte. Finally, thanks to excavations in 1978-81 and the availability of radio-carbon dating techniques, it was pronounced to have been the defended homestead of a local tribe of around 60 BC.

The massive earthwork at Rispain

Wigtown

Until it was designated Scotland's official National Book Town in 1997 (see below), the county's (theoretical) capital had lost much of its sense of purpose. Yet its history is deep and long, and by comparison the more flourishing settlements of Stranraer and Newton Stewart are mere upstarts. Wigtown, with a **castle** and a Dominican **convent** (now both long gone), was already a significant burgh by the thirteenth century.

Its former civic self-esteem is gloriously represented in the (triangular!) Square by the swanky **County Buildings** of 1862-63, made of Cumbrian sandstone in a style based on French and Flemish architecture of the Middle Ages. There had been at least two previous municipal buildings on the site. Both were of the traditional multi-purpose 'tolbooth' type, simultaneously a public meeting-place, a fiscal headquarters and a jail. A prison cell from the last tolbooth was incorporated into the present building.

The building should more accurately be called a town hall. Naming it the 'County Buildings' was a bit of a sop to Wigtonian pride, for in fact when Wigtownshire County Council was still in operation (before local government re-organisation in 1975) the real power was in Stranraer. Its principal function became judicial but even that was steadily whittled away, the sheriff court closing in 1975 and even the lowly district court being taken away in 1998. The building was extensively refurbished for the new millennium and the oddest of its current functions is relaying to visitors live pictures of an ospreys' nest.

In the Square it is easy to forget that Wigtown's former prosperity was based on being a **port**. A trip down Harbour Road, off South Main Street, is evocative of this almost forgotten maritime past, when schooners took away agricultural exports and the *Countess of Galloway* steamer would call on her way to Liverpool. A new quay was built in 1818 following a change in the course of the River Bladnoch. The harbour records for 1832 show that 160 vessels used the port.

Wigtown's once busy but now disused harbour

The coming of the railways in the second half of the nineteenth century undermined the old economy of Wigtown and by the early twentieth century the harbour was almost deserted. The Galloway guide-book author C H Dick reported that he had found just 'one small rowing boat'. Around the same time, another local writer observed: 'It is hardly one's idea of a county town in a bustling age. And, indeed, most of the county business is transacted in the larger centres of Stranraer and Newton-Stewart. It is only on special occasions, such as election times, that Wigtown asserts its position as the metropolis of the county.'

The Galloway novelist S R Crockett had his own way of expressing the placidity of the county town, which he thought more accurate to call the 'county village': 'its square seems permanently hushed as for an open-air communion'. But that was the quality that attracted him to Wigtown: 'The tall trees where the rooks had once their homes, and so annoyed the burgesses, please me beyond words. If I had to live in any town, it would be Wigtown – especially if they would let the crows come back to their ancient dwellings.'

The English travel writer H V Morton visited Wigtown in the early 1930s while researching *In Scotland Again* (1933). He found it to be 'like all Galloway towns, as neat and swept as a town can be.' But he was also struck by how quiet it was, indeed 'rather solemn'. He put this down to the decline in its maritime role:

> The death of a harbour always withdraws a seaport from the world and spreads through its streets an air of bereavement. As a mother will in silence mourn a child, so places like Wigtown mourn their vanished ships. The mind of Wigtown seems to be cast back into other times. Perhaps so much happened to it during its youth that nothing can surprise or interest it now.

John Everett Millais' painting *The Martyr of the Solway* (1871) is testimony to the story's enduring poignancy

Wigtown's most frequently told story is a particularly repellent one. It is of the two seventeenth-century women known as the **Wigtown Martyrs**, victims in 1685 of the vicious government repression of the Covenanters who were fighting against an English Episcopalian takeover of the Scots Kirk. They were put to death in the cruellest of ways, by being tied to stakes in the River Bladnoch and slowly drowned as the tide came in.

The women were found guilty of attending outlawed open-air services known as conventicles. At first there were four accused. One gained her freedom by recanting; another, thirteen years of age, was excused on the grounds of her immaturity. That left 63-year-old Margaret Maclauchlan and 18-year-old Margaret Wilson. The stake for the older woman was placed closer to the incoming tide in the hope that her suffering would encourage the younger one to renounce her convictions in time to be reprieved, but the tactic was to no avail.

A memorial marks the site where the martyrs died. The river has since altered its course and the location is in saltmarsh

S R Crockett featured the Wigtown drownings in his novel *The Men of the Moss-Hags* (1895). After the older woman has succumbed to the tide, the spotlight switches to young Margaret. The emotive scene-setting is in the words of the story's narrator:

> Her great head coverture of hair – which, had I been her lad, I should have delighted to touch and stroke – now broke from the maiden's snood, and fell into the water. There it floated, making a fair golden shining in the grimy tide, like the halo which is about the sun when it rises. Also her face was as the face of an angel, being turned upward to God. Then they began to drive the folk from the sands for fear that they might see the beauty of the dying maid, and go mad with anger at the sight.

Margaret sings the 25th Psalm:

> After the last line there was a break and a silence! And no more – and no more! But after the silence had endured a space, there arose a wailing that went from the hill of Wigtown to the farthest shore of the Cree – the wailing of a whole countryside for a young lass done to death in the flower of her youth, in the untouched grace and favour of her virginity.

There has been some debate over the years about whether the executions were actually carried out. At one point the Privy Council granted a stay of execution and there is no record of what happened after that. On the other hand, the kirk-session minutes of 1711 have an account of both the trial and the execution, and, although that was some time after the event, it was still within living memory. The consensus now among historians is that the

The Martyrs Monument

deaths did in fact take place.

The two Margarets are high in the pantheon of 'martyrs' who died for 'the true religion'. Their story appealed to Victorian sentimentalists. The English artist John Everett Millais painted *The Martyr of the Solway* in 1871. Margaret Wilson would have been horrified to have known that Millais' first version of the picture depicted her naked.

The women's graves are in the kirkyard at Wigtown, and at Windyhill off the town's High Vennel a memorial was erected in the 1858 for them and others 'by whom during the age of persecution our Religion and Liberties as now established were secured, and as a lesson to posterity never to lose or abuse those glorious privileges planted by their labours, rooted in their suffering and watered in their blood'.

In the kirkyard it is almost a relief to turn to the following jolly example of commemorative modesty:

> And his son John of honest fame,
> Of stature small, and a leg lame,
> Content he was with portion small,
> Keeped shop in Wigtown, and that's all.

The **parish kirk** in Bank Street dates mainly from the 1850s but the grounds contain fragments of earlier structures.

With the mechanisation of farming, the closure of local creameries and the mothballing of the nearby whisky distillery (now reopened), Wigtown by the last decade of the twentieth century was in a sorry state. No one could seriously have predicted that the means of regeneration would be found through becoming a **Book Town**.

The original British book town was Hay-on-Wye in Wales. The government agency Scottish Enterprise became involved in investigating the possibility of the phenomenon being replicated north of the Border. A commissioned report from the Scottish Tourism

Research Unit at the University of Strathclyde concluded that 'a book town might provide a major opportunity for economic development and be a flagship tourism and cultural development for a rural town in Scotland'.

There was a national competition. Wigtown, which already had one outstandingly good second-hand bookshop, applied along with five other towns. Wigtown's business plan was judged to be the most impressive and in 1997 victory came its way. The following year Wigtown Book Town was formally launched. Its status differs from that of all the other book towns that have sprung up – in Belgium, France, the Netherlands and the USA as well as Hay-on-Wye. The rest are self-declared; Wigtown is the first and only one to be an official nomination.

Within a few years the number of bookshops and other book-related businesses had risen to about thirty. 'When I first drove into Wigtown,' said one of the first to set up shop in the new Book Town, 'I remember looking around and saying, "What a strange place. So grand and so derelict."' In 1999 a South of Scotland MSP told the Scottish Parliament that 'at one time [pre-Book Town] Wigtown looked

like something out of a western, with tumbleweed blowing down the street...The buildings were literally falling down.'

The year-round trade from visiting bibliophiles is boosted in the late autumn by the annual Wigtown Book Festival. Efforts are made to give the festival events a novel slant, as in 2006: 'We have one of the leading actresses from the Cannes Film Festival – Kate Dickie – being interviewed by the local farmer and Louis de Bernieres being interviewed by the Wigtown butcher.'

With Wigtown now being such a literary place, it is particularly apt that a hotel in South Main Street has been re-named after the novel *Wigtown Ploughman*, the most celebrated piece of writing ever to have emerged from the Machars. The library in the County Buildings has also been named after its author John McNeillie, aka Ian Niall (see Part 2 – The Writers).

James Robertson Justice (1907-75), the comic movie actor best known for playing Sir Lancelot Spratt in *Doctor in the House* (1954), was one of the more kenspeckle residents of Wigtown in the 1940s. At first, during the Second World War, he rented a cottage between Wigtown and Newton Stewart; after the war he bought a house called Orchardton in Wigtown itself. The locals knew him as 'Beardie'. The Machars was the ideal location in which to pursue his ornithological interests. He didn't just like observing birds. As a passionate wildfowler, he liked catching them too and claimed to have invented a rocket-propelled net for the purpose.

Robertson Justice's English public school-educated uppercrustiness belied his Socialism; in 1950 he contested the North Angus and Mearns parliamentary constituency for the Labour Party (unsuccessfully). He justified ostentatiously driving around in a Rolls-Royce by promising to turn it into an armoured car for

'The Revolution'. In 1950 he sold his Wigtown property, and from then on his career took off, beginning with a spell in Hollywood. While still a Wigtownee, however, he was already a familiar face on the big screen. In the town's pubs he was no doubt appreciated above all for his appearance in *Whisky Galore* (1948).

To the north-west of Wigtown, the **Torhousekie Stone Circle**, though not exactly a Stonehenge or a Callanish, is nonetheless a very impressive and surprisingly well preserved group of stones from possibly the second millennium BC. The circle consists of nineteen granite boulders, increasing in height from north-west to south-east. Three more boulders are in the middle. Various other stones nearby may be related. Theories abound. A ritualistic meeting-place? A funeral parlour? A key to the calendar? It used to be thought of as the tomb of King Galdus, alternatively known as Aldus MacGaldus (a likely one). Frankly, no one knows.

Part Two

THEMES and PERSONALITIES

The Early History

In the beginning, of course, there was no 'Wigtownshire' nor 'Galloway' nor 'Scotland' (though for convenience these terms must inevitably be used before their times). There was just unnamed sea-girt territory, released from the grip of the final Ice Age, onto which **nomads** from more southerly parts migrated probably between seven and eight thousand years ago. The warming of the climate had given the land an almost impenetrably thick cover of trees and vegetation, and so these early settlers developed their communities by the shore, along the fringes of Wigtown Bay, Luce Bay and Loch Ryan. With implements made from stone, animal bone and antlers, they gathered wild food, caught fish and hunted for animals in the forests.

It took another couple of thousand years for **agriculture** to evolve. These farmers, from about 4000 BC onwards, were the people who left behind the big stone monuments of which Wigtownshire has such a rich heritage: burial chambers like those on the moors around New Luce and mysterious megaliths like the Torhousekie Stone Circle near Wigtown and the Drumtroddan standing-stones near Port William.

Another puzzling legacy of these later stages of the Stone Age are the so-called **'cup-and-ring markings'**, carvings on outcrops of rock in the fields, which are characteristic of Galloway as a whole and are particularly prevalent in the Shire at Drumtroddan and at Balcraig near Monreith. The precise function of these cup and ring shapes still eludes even the most earnest research and speculation. Ronald W B Morris's *The Prehistoric Rock Art of Galloway & The Isle of Man* (1979) catalogues no fewer than one hundred and four theories attempting to explain their origin, giving each proposition points out of ten for plausibility. The theory that the incisions record the sexual conquests of the local chieftain is, a little disappointingly, awarded *nil* points.

From around 2000 BC, the concept of ore-smelting having evolved, the basis of technology was moving from stone to **metal**. At first it was copper, followed by the discovery of bronze, a tougher alloy of copper and tin. The final stage in the development of prehistoric metal-working came around the start of the first millennium BC with the introduction of iron. Many of these advances came with the northward migration of **Celts** from continental Europe.

This **Iron Age culture** of the Celts is the first in the history of the Solway region to become, from our own point of view, recognisably human. We know of the language they spoke, which we term Brittonic; and we can still see where they made their homes and deduce from the evidence what their living conditions were like. In whatever direction you look across the landscape of Wigtownshire today, you will have no difficulty spotting at least one or two of the many hilltop sites where they built their timber and turf **forts**. The Shire's best known example is Rispain Camp near Whithorn. Other forts were built on seaside promontories, like Barsalloch Point on the east coast of Luce Bay (see Part 1 – Monreith). Most ingenious of all their homesteads were the artificial loch-dwellings known as **crannogs**, several of which were spectacularly exposed in the nineteenth century when Dowalton Loch near Whauphill was drained. From this period there is even, at Ardwell Point on the west coast of the south Rhins and also near Stairhaven, the remains of **brochs**, tall circular drystone buildings of a type more commonly found in the north of Scotland.

Such, then, was the settled population of south-west Scotland when, during the first century AD, the **Romans**, having extended their empire into southern Britannia, came north to reconnoitre the native cultures of Caledonia. They named the people of the south-west the **Novantae**. Although the Romans never formed any permanent bases here, they certainly knew all about Wigtownshire. They surveyed it, mapped it, and assessed the opportunities for using it as the springboard for a conquest of Ireland. The prospect of nipping across the channel from the west coast of the Rhins must indeed have been an exceedingly tempting one. But, in the end, they decided against it and their active interest in this northern hinterland of the Solway spread little beyond their *de facto* western frontier at the valley of the Fleet in Kirkcudbrightshire.

The inhabitants of Wigtownshire were fully aware, both before and after the completion of Hadrian's Wall in the year 127, of the Romans' proximity. There was, after all, plenty of trading between locals and incomers, as the discovery of imperial coins at Sandhead has shown; and, in some cases, scions of the native ruling elites chose to advance themselves through enlisting in the Roman army.

The early tribes of Galloway, allegedly inspired by the Roman wall from the Solway to Tyneside, were long thought to have built a version of their own to inhibit invasions from the north. Supposed fragments of it are still marked on some maps as the **Deil's Dyke**.

The theory that they all got together and created a solid northern frontier has been an archaeological wild-goose-chase for centuries. Joseph Train (1779-1852), Ayrshire exciseman turned Galloway antiquarian, fuelled the speculation by writing a detailed account of his tramps along what he claimed was an eighty-mile defensive rampart from Loch Ryan in the west to Dumfriesshire in the east. Today the theory is put down as wishful thinking. Geoffrey Stell, a veteran inspector for the Royal Commission on the Ancient and Historical Monuments of Scotland, jocularly dismisses the alleged construction as 'Train's Dyke', concluding that it has 'no existence in fact, being a disconnected series of tracks or local and late boundaries with no common structural character'.

Yet the concept of a northern defensive barrier has been so alluring to historians that even as relatively recently as the 1960s John F Robertson, in *The Story of Galloway*, not only gives it credence but also adds his own fanciful detail:

> The Galloway tribal chieftains met to discuss how they could combat this continual threat...they remembered the defensive methods of their old masters, the Romans. A wall was the answer...Plans for the wall were drawn up and dimensions agreed upon.

Perhaps Robertson should have learned some scepticism from the guide-book author C H Dick, who had written some sixty years earlier about his own difficulties in trying to find the so-called Deil's Dyke:

> Whatever may have been the value of the dyke to the ancient inhabitants of Galloway, one may look for little help in identifying it from those of the present day. A farmer of whom I made inquiry near Kirkcalla [west of Loch Ochiltree] told me that he had lived there all his life and knew nothing about it, and a shepherd boy directed my attention to what were manifestly the ruins of a modern dry-stone wall.

In historical terms Wigtownshire's greatest claim to fame is as Scotland's **'cradle of Christianity'**. The romantic setting of Scotland's other great Christian nursery, the island of Iona off the north-west mainland, has tended to steal the limelight from the truly pioneering priests who formed an evangelising centre of operations at Whithorn in the fifth century, either soon after or just before the retreat of the Romans in the early 400s. The sacred stones of Kirkmadrine (see Part 1 – Sandhead) and those in the collection of the Priory Museum at Whithorn are ample testimony to the presence here of a Christian community a generation or so before the celebrated Irishman Columba arrived on Iona.

Much mystery surrounds the exact identity of **Ninian**, Wigtownshire's very own saintly star. The traditional account (unreliably based on chronicles composed centuries later) asserts that he was the son of a local Brittonic chieftain, that he went to Rome for clerical training and that, when he returned home in 397, he founded his 'Candida Casa' [Latin, 'white house'] church at Whithorn as a base from which to spread the good news among the pagan Picts of the north. Modern scholarship is more sceptical, however, and there are now question marks over the period during which Ninian is supposed to have operated and even over whether such a man ever operated at all! There is even a suggestion that there may have been two Ninians, one in the fifth century, another in the sixth.

No such uncertainties, however, inhibited the growth of an enormous Ninian cult. Whithorn became throughout the Middle Ages a major place of Christian pilgrimage. Along the coast spiritual reception-centres developed: St Ninian's Chapel at the Isle of Whithorn and Chapel Finian on the east side of Luce Bay (see Part 1 – Port William) are examples. A visit to the shrine of Ninian was a favourite way for Scotland's battle-scarred monarchs to salve their heavy consciences. In the fourteenth century Robert I, the victor of Bannockburn, made the pilgrimage during his preparation for death, and from the 1490s until he perished at the Battle of Flodden in 1513 James IV was frequently in the Machars, characteristically combining spiritual business with earthly pleasure (see Part 1 – Whithorn).

Conversion to Christianity was not the only major development after the departure of the occupiers from the Italian peninsula. The Roman abandonment of Britannia left the field clear for any marauding migrants who fancied taking their chances around the Solway basin. There was no shortage of armed opportunists. They were all the usual suspects of Dark Ages history and they came from all airts.

The first to fill the power vacuum, from the opposite side of the Solway, was the Cumbrian kingdom of **Rheged**. This was less a takeover than a re-affirmation of a common Celtic culture, with a shared Brittonic language (the forerunner of modern Welsh), which had been split apart by the Roman command of the area around what is now Carlisle. The influence of Rheged may well be reflected in the name 'Dunragit'.

Rheged eventually succumbed to the westward expansionism of the **Angles**, the Germanic people from across the North Sea who founded the kingdom of Northumbria and would later be the basis for the evolution of England. Without entirely eliminating the pre-existing tribal society of the northern Solway, the Angles took control of the area throughout most of the seventh and eighth centuries. They re-built the church at Whithorn, both physically and spiritually, creating a new bishopric of their own.

By the ninth century the Angles were pulling back towards their territories in the east and south of Britain, having lost the initiative to the **Vikings** of Norway and Denmark, for whom the Solway was a natural extension of the western seaboard of which by now they were the masters. All the while, off and on, batches of **Irish** migrants had been crossing the water and creating scattered communities of their own. The language which the Irish brought with them, Gaelic (a Celtic cousin of Brittonic), would eventually supercede all the other migrant tongues of this period and profoundly affect in perpetuity the naming of Wigtownshire's topography.

The process of forming the bedrock population of medieval Galloway was not over yet. A final, defining phase of migration brought the **Gall Gaidheil**. They too were Gaelic-speaking and their name means either 'stranger Gael' or 'Scandanavian Gael'. As the term suggests, they were a hybrid people, a genetic mixture that emerged from the mingling of sea-faring warriors operating along the great maritime highway stretching from Ireland to Iceland. By the tenth century the Gall Gaidheil were thoroughly settled in what are now Wigtownshire and Kirkcudbrightshire and from their name evolved the term 'Galloway' that still defines those two counties collectively.

By the early 1100s Galloway was almost a nation in its own right, a small but powerful wedge between Scotland to its north and England to its south. It had its own line of hereditary rulers whose western stronghold was Cruggleton Castle near Garlieston. Historians call them the **Lords of Galloway** but they thought of themselves as more monarchs than just local magnates and were rather fond of flaunting the description *rex Galwitensium* [Latin, 'king of the Gallovidians']. Their prestige was founded on military capability, particularly their formidable naval presence around the Irish Sea. They were therefore supremely useful to their larger neighbours as suppliers of mercenary fighters.

Through astute marital alliances they kept themselves well connected with all the power-bases of the British and Irish isles. **Fergus**, the first of these lords to be known to us by name, was married to an illegitimate daughter of Henry I of England, while his own daughter Affreca married the king of Mann [Isle of Man]. The last of them, **Alan**, married a niece of the Scottish king, thus establishing a royal blood-line that would later bring his grandson John Balliol to the Scottish throne (albeit ignominiously). Alan's wife also brought to this partnership an extensive property portfolio in the south of England. The numerous offspring of successive Lords were particularly adept at marrying into the Anglo-Norman landed gentry that increasingly infiltrated much of Britain after William of Normandy's conquest of England in 1066.

Alan's rule epitomised the pick-and-choose political wiliness of the Galloway lordship. While maintaining his Solway fiefdom as much as possible as a land apart, he nonetheless enjoyed privileged access to the royal courts of both Scotland and England. Indeed Alan had such a close association with King John of England that he is specifically named in the preamble to the most famous legal document in English history, the Magna Carta of 1215.

The Lordship of Galloway survived through four generations of leaders into the thirteenth century. But a burgeoning Scotland was edging steadily closer. Every time there was a political problem in Galloway, as there was disastrously during the ultimately fratricidal rivalry between Fergus's heirs **Gilbert** and **Uchtred**, the Scottish monarchy seized the opportunity to intervene. Step by step the independence of the province drained away.

Galloway's self-ruling dynasty finally petered out when Alan died in 1234 without a legitimate male heir. From the grassroots there was armed resistance in support of the inheritance claim of Alan's illegitimate son Thomas, but the campaign was a failure. Exploiting what they believed to be their overlordship, the Scots again intervened, this time decisively. Thomas was captured and imprisoned until he was too old to be of any trouble. Henceforth Galloway was effectively absorbed into Scotland. To help maintain its hold the new regime created the Sheriffdom of Wigtown, a jurisdiction covering all of the territory west of the River Cree. The concept of 'Wigtownshire' [shire=sheriffdom] was born!

Becoming part of the newly expanded Scotland did not inaugurate for Wigtownshire a period of peace and prosperity: far from it, for the long and bloody **Wars of Independence** were soon underway. Scotland's chronic instability, exacerbated by internecine conflict over the monarchical succession, gave England ample opportunity over the next one hundred years to test her claim of overlordship in relation to her northern neighbour. When the army of King Edward I, 'Hammer of the Scots', crossed the border in 1296, the castles of both Wigtown and Cruggleton were taken. Stage one of the Scots' resistance campaign ended in the humiliation of capture and hanging for their leader, 'Braveheart' William Wallace. Robert Bruce then took up the cudgels and, thanks to a Scots victory at the Battle of Bannockburn in 1314, the English were deported. In Wigtownshire this turn of events was taken with a pinch of salt, though, for the folk had not forgotten that the Bruces were a gang of Anglo-Norman interlopers and Ayrshire chancers.

For at least another couple of centuries 'wars of independence' between Scotland and England carried on in one form or another. In many respects Wigtownshire was able to remain aloof from all of this conflict. For thing, the county was well away from the usual theatres of war. For another, its controlling landowners – the Adairs, the Kennedys, the McDoualls, the Maxwells and the Stewarts - had other business to be getting on with, which was fighting amongst themselves. The fifteenth and sixteenth centuries saw a massive programme of **castle-building**. These fortifications were put up for defence not against the 'Auld Enemy' in the south but against their very own neighbours.

Even the **Agnews** of Lochnaw (see Part 1 – Leswalt) were not above a spot of skulduggery in the cause of their own self-aggrandisement. I say 'even', because the Agnews were supposed to be the custodians of the law. In the 1450s King James II appointed Andrew Agnew as the first of the **Hereditary Sheriffs**. Strange though it may seem to us now, this jurisdictional post was handed down from father to son across twelve generations of the Agnew family, the only serious interruption in this genetic chain of command being during the Covenanter 'Killing Time' of the 1680s (see below). The family-run Sheriffdom survived even the disgrace of Patrick Agnew in the early sixteenth century. He was found guilty in 1509 of accepting a bribe to acquit a murderer, and four years later he was convicted of oppressing tenants and neighbours and of stealing cows.

The hereditary principle in Wigtownshire was finally ended in 1747. The last of the family sheriffs was Sir Andrew Agnew (died 1771), who received the then extremely generous sum of £4000 as compensation for loss of office.

The history of this judicial function was written by one of their nineteenth-century descendents, another Sir Andrew. His first stab at the subject, *The Agnews of Lochnaw: a History of the Hereditary Sheriffs of Galloway* came out in 1864. It contained numerous inaccuracies and, just before his death, Sir Andrew completed a more trustworthy second edition, *The Hereditary Sheriffs of Galloway* (1893). In it he acknowledges the peculiarity of justice by accident-of-birth but at the same time he is wistful over what was lost after its abolition:

> Thus ended the days of heritable jurisdiction in Scotland. Responsible judicial offices were no longer to be handed down irresponsibly from father to son; and no rational person can now doubt that the change was a wise one.
>
> But this conviction only grew gradually upon the nation. The very classes who might have been thought to be aggrieved at the action of feudal courts, which were notoriously often partial and unfair, were by no means delighted at the change.
>
> They 'aye preferred gentlemen's law' was the style by which they expressed a preference for seeing the magisterial bench presided over by those to whom they yielded an instinctive deference, rather than by more learned strangers. Ignoring the fact that heritable functionaries also derived emoluments from their offices, a Galloway proverb hurls contempt at the stipendiaries with fixed incomes for their services in the disdainful phrase: 'It's no' for nought the gled [hawk] whistles'.

Agnew claims that, although a hereditary judiciary could sometimes show bias, its faults were no worse than those of the higher courts at the time, and that local knowledge could lead to empathy for the victims of national political oppression:

> In such days as those of the Test and Conventicle Act, mere government officials would have hunted out and shot down the poor Covenanters like so many vermin. Not so the feudal magistrates. In almost every instance...the hereditary officials, even at the risk of incurring penalties themselves, exerted themselves to mitigate the rigours of the law, and minimise the sentences against the proscribed. And this, be it remarked, quite apart from any approval of the principles of those condemned.

Sir Andrew lyricises to his conclusion: 'And so it happened not unnaturally that the west country Whigs – the wild Scots of Galloway – had little of the feeling of Levellers [an eighteenth-century protest movement against drystane-dykes] in the matter of feudal privilege, and grieved to see the old baronial edifice tottering to its fall.'

It is interesting to note that, at the close of the Agnew reign, the first *stipendiary* sheriff to be appointed for Wigtownshire was Alexander Boswell, an Ayrshire lawyer and father of James Boswell, famous biographer of the lexicographer and literary heavyweight Dr Samuel Johnson. Boswell resigned from the post after a couple of years and later, as Lord Auchinleck, became a high court judge.

Just as the anarchic habit of battering the brains out of each other was starting to die out in Wigtownshire and there seemed to be a prospect of more civilised living, along came another pretext for fighting in a futile cause. This time it was over **religion**, and before too long saintly Ninian's 'cradle of Christianity' was turned into a cauldron of barbarous bigotry that would not finally be extinguished for another century.

Scotland officially became **Protestant** in 1560 and, with Mary Queen of Scots' fateful flight from the country in 1568, the Catholic menace was finally eliminated. Of course the first priority for Wigtownshire's powerful families was to see what was in it for them. Thus the break-up of the old religious foundations turned into an unseemly land-grab. None were more rapacious than the Kennedys (from 1509 the Earls of Cassilis), an Ayrshire clan with a particularly fat finger in the Wigtownshire pie. In highly dubious circumstances they seized control of a large chunk of ecclesiastical land, most notably that belonging to Glenluce Abbey.

As far as the peasantry were concerned, poverty, remoteness and the general misery of their lives seemed to engender a strong wish for the certainty of salvation, and in the Shire the dogmatic doctrines of John Knox and the other Reformation leaders found ready adherence. Unfortunately, James VI, while embracing Protestantism, favoured the retention of the old Episcopal hierarchy, a concept that the Presbyterians of the new Kirk of Scotland looked upon as a corrupt Papist abomination. The seeds of conflict had been sown.

The 1603 **Union of the Crowns**, under which James VI of Scotland also became James I of England, brought about an escalation in the tension over religious observance. James and his Stuart successors Charles I and Charles II (Scottish by name, English by inclination) had a pig-headed obsession with cementing the unity of the new greater kingdom by means of uniformity of worship, which in practice meant the imposition onto the Kirk of the procedures of the Church of England. What the Scots Presbyterians saw as 'the true religion' was to be polluted by forms of worship redolent of 'Popery'. The crunch came in 1637 with the attempt to introduce into Scottish kirks the English prayer-book. Opposition was expressed by the mass signing of the **National Covenant** in the following year. King and Covenanters took up arms against each other in what became known as the Bishops' Wars.

Wigtownshire was associated with two of the leading clerical protagonists, one from each side of the ideological divide. **John Livingstone** (1603-1672), an immensely popular preacher who was minister at Stranraer for a time, was delegated to take copies of the National Covenant to London and in subsequent years, before finally going into exile in the Netherlands, participated at a high level in negotiations with the Covenanters' opposition. On the other hand **Thomas Sydserff**, who was appointed Bishop of Galloway in 1635 was, as his acceptance of the post suggests, a careerist compromiser, whose endorsement of the Royal policy led to his being publicly reviled and frequently physically attacked. One of his opponents described him as 'a violent, virulent man, a great urger of conformity'. Another of his enemies lampooned him as 'Galloway Tam, that squint-eyed stridling asse'.

The impasse was not resolved even by the beheading of Charles I in 1649 during the English Civil War. The Covenanters formed an alliance with the English parliamentarians but were betrayed, as they were again by Charles II after the Restoration of 1660, despite the monarch's earlier promises while waiting in the wings during the Interregnum. From the early 1660s the situation got steadily worse. On the orders of the King unyielding Presbyterian ministers were ousted from their posts throughout the Shire and replaced by Episcopalian lickspittles. The clerical refuseniks and their congregations took to the hills and worshipped according to their own precepts at open-air meetings known as 'conventicles'.

The government response to this popular defiance was vicious and it culminated in an armed suppression during the 1680s that came to be known as the 'Killing Time'. Of the army officers sent to deal with the dissidents of the south-west, one name stands out in the demonology of Covenanter history: **Sir John Graham of Claverhouse**, later created Viscount Dundee for services to the crown. His dashing good looks earned him the nickname 'Bonnie Dundee' (the title also of a popular Scots song about him) but Wigtownshire prefers to remember him as 'Bluidy Clavers'. The Agnew family were temporarily toppled from their hereditary Sheriffdom (see above) and Claverhouse took control throughout the county, turning the Castle of St John in Stranraer into the command centre for his campaign of coercion.

This period is vividly brought to life by the Dumfriesshire novelist R W McKenna in *Flower o' the Heather* (1922). His hero is an Oxford undergraduate unwittingly recruited by the government troops but soon disillusioned by what he sees:

> In my ignorance, I had thought that when we set out from Dumfries to march through Galloway we should find, opposed to us somewhere, a force of Covenanters who would give battle. I had imagined that these rebels would have an army of their own ready to challenge the forces of the King: but soon I learned that our warfare was an inglorious campaign against unarmed men and women.

Some eighty 'martyrs' were killed across the south-west. The situation in Wigtownshire was so tense that local landowner Sir James Dalrymple (later 1st Viscount Stair – see Celebrities of the Shire), who had spoken up for the rights of his oppressed tenants, felt compelled to seek political asylum in the Netherlands.

If the Covenanters were the 'goodies' in the story of the 'Killing Time' (a moot point given their unattractively hard-faced fundamentalism), **Sir Robert Grierson of Lag** (in Dumfriesshire) was another of the government 'baddies'. It was he who was credited with being in command in 1685 when, with hideously sadistic cruelty, two female dissenters were tied to stakes at the mouth of the River Bladnoch and slowly drowned by the incoming tide, thus ensuring for them perpetual veneration as the 'Wigtown Martyrs' (see Part 1 – Wigtown).

The whole sordid business of Crown versus Covenanters finally came to an end with the so-called **Glorious Revolution** of 1689 when the last of the Stuart kings, the Catholic James VII and II, was deposed and replaced by William of Orange and his wife, James's daughter Mary. From then on the Presbyterians of Wigtownshire and of Scotland as a whole were left in peace to follow their dogma in a style of their choice.

In the following century, when the Stuarts attempted to regain the throne through the **Jacobite Risings** of 1715 and 1745, the folk of Wigtownshire had no enthusiasm for the cause of the 'Old Pretender' James and his son, the 'Young Pretender' Charles. They remembered only too well the damage that the insensitive rule of their ancestors had inflicted on the Shire. Only one Wigtownshire landowner, Basil Hamilton of Baldoon, joined the abortive 1715 insurrection and he paid dearly for his folly. His estates were confiscated and he himself would have been executed had it not been for the mitigating intervention of a well-connected relative.

There is an intriguing Wigtownshire connection with an earlier anti-Jacobite crackdown. The Scottish secretary of state who ordered the infamous Massacre of Glencoe in 1692 was John Dalrymple, later 1st Earl of Stair (see Celebrities of the Shire).

The formal **Union** of Scotland and England in 1707, when the Scottish parliamentarians voted to join a new London-based British legislature, brought to the folk of Wigtownshire no immediately apparent benefits. All they saw at first was a rise in taxation. They were already well practised in the dark arts of **smuggling** and now they had no qualms about moving into it on an even larger scale. All sectors of society were united in their conviction that tax avoidance, particularly when the tax in question was 'foreign', was every Scot's patriotic duty. Even the kirk ministers endorsed their murky work – so long as it did not take place on the Sabbath, of course! The smuggling became so endemic to the economy of the county that they were still at it in the closing years of the eighteenth century. In the 1780s a traveller arriving in Galloway sensed an apparent lack of trade and asked how the people managed to make a living. 'Och, we smuggle a bit' was the reply.

The 'bit', however, was a big one. Wine and brandy were brought in illicitly from southern Europe, rum from the Caribbean, tobacco from Virginia and salt from Ireland. The Isle of Man was pivotal in the operation and, being so close to this offshore staging-post, Wigtownshire was an ideal part of the mainland for the receipt of the contraband and its distribution to the inland markets.

There was hardly an indentation along the western seaboard of the Rhins and around the fringe of Luce Bay that was not at some time in use as a secret landing-place. Caves were used for temporary storage; so too were ingenious 'brandy-holes' within domestic and farm buildings. The shore around Port William was particularly notorious. At the farm of Drumtroddan a fireproof storage chamber was built under the farm kiln, which was lit whenever the customs officers were known to be in the vicinity (see Part 1 – Port William). Even the vaults of old Sinniness Castle near Stairhaven found a new purpose.

Official efforts to clamp down were largely ineffective in the face of overwhelming popular support for the smugglers. In 1774 the magistrates and town council of Wigtown agreed to set an example by deciding 'to unanimously resolve that, for the future, we will not drink any French brandy, either in our own houses or in others, whatsoever'. But their resolve had no effect on the populace. The revenue service was inadequately staffed and the smuggling gangs were often able to carry on their business in open defiance of the authorities. An exciseman later recalled an incident on the outskirts of Wigtown in the 1770s when 210 horses laden with contraband passed by with impunity, despite the presence of customs officers and some thirty soldiers.

In the early years of the nineteenth century a re-organised customs and revenue service became much more aggressively concerted in its surveillance and prosecution, and in time the smuggling habit died out. But the government's most effective weapon against the contraband trade was the policy of simply eliminating its original motivation by gradually reducing import duties.

The Shire's history of smuggling is neatly summed up by the novelist Sir Walter Scott in a footnote to *Guy Mannering* (1815):

> In those halcyon days of the free trade, the fixed price for carrying a box of tea, or bale of tobacco, from the coast of Galloway to Edinburgh, was fifteen shillings, and a man with two horses carried four such packages. The trade was entirely destroyed by Mr. Pitt's celebrated commutation law, which, by reducing the duties upon excisable articles, enabled the lawful dealer to compete with the smuggler. The statute was called in Galloway and Dumfries-shire, by those who had thriven upon the contraband trade, 'the burning and starving act'.

In many ways the old pre-Union way of life in a corner of Scotland that was so far removed from the centres of power carried on. But in at least one respect the county was undergoing profound changes throughout the eighteenth century. This was the agrarian revolution that turned subsistence farming into an industry geared to the efficient creation of tradeable surpluses. In the process the raw land of Wigtownshire evolved into the orderly landscape as we know it today. That will be one of the themes of the chapter that follows.

The Land and the Sea

An author who was appearing at the Wigtown Book Festival publicly complained about how difficult it had been to get to the venue, that the most feasible route from his starting-point of Edinburgh had been to fly all the way to Belfast in Northern Ireland and then take the ferry back to Wigtownshire, a roundabout journey that no doubt would have reinforced the outsider's view that the Shire is in the 'back-of-beyond'. Certainly, to anyone having to use today's degenerate public transport, the south-west corner of Scotland will indeed seem to be relatively remote. As far as mainland Scotland is concerned, it is, quite literally, peripheral.

But take a fresh look at the map, think not land but ***sea***, and Wigtownshire starts to appear more like the very heart of the British Isles. Which is exactly what it was for thousands of years, from the very earliest human migrations right up to the middle of the nineteenth century, before the development of the railway system (see below) turned transportation from mainly maritime to predominantly land-based.

Follow the county's wonderfully varied indented coastline and you will not go far before coming across evidence of old berthing facilities. From these, sailing ships and later steamers had easy access north to Clydeside and the Hebrides, west to Ireland and south to the Isle of Man and the important English ports of Whitehaven and Liverpool, as well to more distant destinations like France and Spain, the Americas, and the countries around the Baltic Sea. Many of the harbours are now disused. With the exception of the Loch Ryan ports servicing the cross-channel ferries (see The Irish Connection), the quaysides that are still in operation are now catering mainly for the recreational market, though, as the world carbon crisis becomes more acute, the notion of barques, brigantines, sloops and schooners one day re-appearing in these waters can no longer be dismissed as a wistful fantasy.

Once upon an unimaginably long time ago it was *all* sea. Where Wigtownshire now is was part of what geologists call the **Lapetus Ocean**, which disappeared when two great continents collided. The mud and sand of the ocean floor are now the four-hundred-and-sixty-million-year-old sedimentary rocks on which the Wigtownshire landscape rests. Look at the folded rock formations on the coast around the Isle of Whithorn or along the western shore of Luce Bay north of the Mull of Galloway and you are seeing evidence of the Caledonian Orogeny, the mountain-building period set off by that great continental collision.

The subsequent movement across the land of **glaciers** had a defining effect on the final appearance of the Wigtownshire terrain. Glacial erosion wore down the original mountains and left a trail of detritus, which, in the case of Wigtownshire, was the basis of the characteristic knobbliness of its undulating Machars and Rhins. In Scotland these knolls and hillocks are generally referred to as drums [from Gaelic *druim*, 'ridge']. But in Galloway we prefer to call them, rather cutely, drumlins.

When the glaciers melted at the close of the final Ice Age, another characteristic feature of Wigtownshire was formed. The change in sea level created **raised beaches**, examples of which are common along the eastern shore of both Luce Bay and Loch Ryan. As a whole the Wigtownshire coastline is extraordinarily varied, from the spectacular cliffs along the west coast of the Rhins to the ever-changing sand-dune complex of Torrs Warren at the top of Luce Bay, from shores both rocky and sandy to the saltmarshes of Wigtown Bay. All of these features provide habitats for an amazing range of bird life. The cliffs are thronged with guillemots, puffins, razorbills and kittiwakes; the dunes and marshlands host vast numbers of wintering geese; the Scaur rocks out in Luce Bay are renowned for their dense colonies of gannets.

Thanks to its south-westerly position and to the effects of the Gulf Stream, Wigtownshire's climate is relatively mild and damp, ideal conditions for growing grass. And so the grazing of **livestock** has long been the mainstay of its agriculture: beef cattle at first, but later a big move into dairying.

Even as early as the first half of the sixteenth century the county already had a reputation as a 'store of bestiall'. It was like a vast lush reserve for the fattening of cattle before they were taken long distances to the markets, mainly south of the Border where greater affluence and bigger populations created demand. It was not just local livestock that were prepared upon the Wigtownshire pastureland. Cattle dealers also processed imported beasts from Ireland.

Until the development of efficient steamships the animals in effect provided their own bulk transport across hundreds of miles to their final selling and slaughtering places. They hoofed it! The technical term is '**droving**', the guiding of huge herds along dedicated routes. Wigtownshire's main drove-road started at Portpatrick and wound its way to the English border via the trysting-places of Glenluce, Newton Stewart, New Galloway and Dumfries. The Wigtownshire cattle droving trade flourished more than most because its excellent pasturage was conveniently situated for the southwards transit.

The area was also well known for having its own **breed of cattle**, the hardy black-coated Galloway. Today it is better known for the strikingly picturesque variant of the breed, the Belted Galloway or Beltie (from the band of white round its middle). The Galloways are well kitted out for bad weather, with an outer coat of long hair to shed the rain and a softer undercoat for warmth.

From medieval times the area was renowned also for a native breed of horse called the **Galloway Nag** (not to be confused with a girning wifie). King Robert Bruce is said to have ridden one during the Battle of Bannockburn in 1314. The fourteenth-century French chronicler Jean Froissart, visiting Scotland in the 1360s, described the Scots going to war: 'The knights and esquires are well mounted on large bay horses, the common people on little Galloways'. William Shakespeare has a comic reference to them in Part 2 of *Henry IV*:

> For God's sake, thrust him down stairs! I cannot endure such a fustian rascal.
> 'Thrust him down stairs'! Know we not Galloway nags?

At first the cattle trade was fairly chaotic and eventually landowners began to appreciate that there would be greater profit if a more organised approach was adopted. Though the movement towards agricultural improvement on a large scale did not get into full swing until the second quarter of the eighteenth century, Wigtownshire had in **Sir David Dunbar** (about 1610-86) an outstanding example of innovativeness well ahead of its time. From the late 1600s, at his Baldoon estate near Bladnoch, he was pioneering the concept of **enclosure** for the more efficient management of breeding, rearing and fattening programmes. This strategy had the additional benefit, to small-time arable farmers, of reducing the notorious incidence of damage to crops from roaming beasts. Dunbar also campaigned for an upgrading of the drove-roads. A local kirk minister described his enterprise:

> Sir David Dunbar of Baldone hath a park about two miles and an half in length and ane mile and a half in breadth, the greatest part whereof is rich and deep valley ground and yields excellent grass. This park can keep in it winter and summer about a thousand bestaill, part of which he buys from the countrey, and grazeth there all winter, the other part whereof is of his own breed.

In general terms pre-1700 farming in Wigtownshire was small-scale, primitive and exceedingly hand-to-mouth in character. Much of the land was hopelessly boggy, while the more promising parts were inefficiently divided into 'rigs' among the numerous occupants of the rural housing clusters known as 'fermtouns'. Sir David Dunbar's vision inspired the following generations to undertake improvements across the whole range of farming activities. Waterlogged land was extensively drained and new crops like potatoes and turnips were introduced.

The **'improving' landowners** were of course the principal beneficiaries of these radical changes. At first the poorer people, dispossessed of their communal grazing, resisted but the anti-enclosure movement that came to be known as the **Levellers** was short-lived. The eighteenth century saw the county fundamentally transformed from crude open pastureland into an ordered landscape of dyked fields, parklands and planned woodlands. Ancillary trades developed in tandem, the increasing prosperity of the cattle trade giving rise, for example, to a proliferation of small tanneries throughout the county.

The central component of this agrarian revolution was the development of new techniques of stone walling, better known locally as **drystane-dyking**, a skill in which Galloway led the way for the rest of Scotland to such an extent that one of the commonest styles of construction was named the Galloway Dyke. To this day the dykes of this period remain the paramount defining feature of the Wigtownshire landscape.

As the Scots term suggests, drystane-dykes are constructed entirely without mortar. Paradoxically, that is why they are so durable. Since mortar disintegrates, any masonry dependent on it will sooner or later become de-stabilised. A drystane-dyke derives its strength from its very structure and typically is capable of standing for hundreds of years.

The pioneer dykers had plenty of building material to hand. The scraping effect of the Ice Age glaciers that had passed across the land had deposited a great deal of stone detritus. These field boulders were supplemented, wherever necessary, from small ad hoc quarries. And there was yet another source of stone, the exploiting of which, were it to happen today, would be a criminal offence. Two hundred years ago there was little sentiment for the artefacts of antiquity. Any castle or kirk no longer in active use was considered to be a potential quarry of ready-cut blocks. As you inspect a dyke you may well be looking at bits of a medieval abbey.

A typical dyke began with a six-inch trench for the foundations made up of tightly packed small flat stones. If, however, a big boulder embedded into the ground was in the proposed line of the dyke, it would be ingeniously incorporated into the structure. A tapering double dyke with infill called hearting was then built on these foundations. Before it had reached the two-feet mark, flat stones large enough to cover the width of the wall plus a slight overhang formed a stabilising through band. Another tapering double dyke with hearting continued upwards, and this was topped by another through band called the cover band. The dyke was then finished off with a row of cope stones. The final height was usually at least four and a half feet but could be anything up to six feet. A common variation is known as the Galloway Hedge: a dyke combined with a hedge of thorns planted to grow through the lower wall and then up the other side.

Though in so many ways the massive industrialisation of Scotland in the nineteenth century passed Wigtownshire by, it did nonetheless have one significant effect on the county's agriculture. The vast new urban populations servicing the mines, the foundries and the factories of central Scotland needed supplies of relatively inexpensive protein and the quick-fix solution was the expansion of **dairy farming** for the production of milk, butter and cheese. Wigtownshire's green and pleasant land was well suited to this vital conversion from beef to milk production, and for the county it was a godsend too, for already its cattle trade was being badly undermined by imports of cheaper meat from other parts of the world.

The first large-scale conversion to dairying in Wigtownshire took place in the early 1800s and from then on the changeover progressed steadily, the farmers of the Shire reluctantly swallowing their pride and finally accepting that the more impressive milk yields came from the breed of cow that takes its name from its northern competitor Ayrshire.

The development of dairy farming in the county inaugurated a fine tradition of **cheese-making**, cheddar becoming the favoured variety. In the early days it was a small-scale operation by hand, every farm having its own cheese-maker. The artisan approach was eventually largely replaced by the more industrial techniques of creameries. Around the beginning of the twentieth century there were some ten of these dotted around the county. Now they too have disappeared. Wigtownshire cheese production is currently concentrated into a single large factory at Stranraer, which was acquired from the Scottish Milk Marketing Board by the Glasgow-based firm McLelland, which in turn was taken over by Lactalis of France. The Stranraer operation is now run under the name of the Caledonian Cheese Company and produces brands such as Seriously Strong, which the company describes as 'a very full, rich, sweet cheddar with hints of caramel'.

Although livestock farming has always predominated, the rich, loamy soil of the Machars was discovered in the eighteenth century to be well suited to the cultivation of **tatties** [Scots, 'potatoes']. The relatively mild climate is kind to the early crops, which would otherwise be liable to damage by frost, and even in this age of factory-processed food the year's first appearance in the shops of Wigtownshire earlies can still cause a wee flutter of epicurean excitement.

Shire tatties are so famous that there is a recipe named after them. 'Wigtown Tatties' are cooked with mushrooms and herbs by the 'stovies' method. Either as an accompaniment or as a meal in themselves, stovies are a classic Scottish dish similar in principle to the French *dauphinois*: ie they are thinly sliced and slow-cooked or sweated over a low heat with minimal liquid. The resemblance to the French technique has led to the theory that the word stovies derives from *etuvier*, 'to stew'. But it may equally derive more straightforwardly from the old Scots/northern English 'to stove' [stew].

Tatties arrived in Galloway in the 1720s but they took a long time to catch on. At first they were cultivated as a novelty in the laird's garden. The peasants resisted them, preferring to feed them to pigs - a prejudice that was not without its benefit, for during the eighteenth century there was a huge increase in Wigtownshire bacon production. By the early nineteenth century, however, tatties had become a major element in the daily domestic diet.

The abundance of good-quality Wigtownshire produce led to the development of **tattie mills** producing starch, flour and, after the introduction of canning technology, *tinned* tatties (yeuk!). The armed forces were the biggest clients. The last splurge of demand came during the First World War, after which the tattie mills went into terminal decline. At the peak of this processing industry there had been tattie mills at Newmilns on the River Bladnoch, at Fordbank near Wigtown and at Elrig, while Stranraer had two of them.

Long before the Shire tattie came into fashion, the county was producing another kind of crop for which it was well known. This was the variety of apple called the **Galloway Pippin**. It has a long pedigree, having been first cultivated in the Middle Ages by the friars of Wigtown. In the nursery catalogues of today it still features, being described as yellow with spots of russet in appearance and strong in flavour.

The success of Wigtownshire's dairy revolution was later accelerated by the expansion of the **railways** into the south-west, which greatly improved the timely transportation of perishables. The Victorian railway system arrived first in eastern Galloway, reaching Castle Douglas in Kirkcudbrightshire in 1859. The westward extension into Wigtownshire, laid in the early 1860s, was known as the Portpatrick Railway. The authorities were still under the illusion that Portpatrick was the most suitable location for the sea connection with Ireland. There were to be two stations there, one for the town, the other for the quayside. However, Portpatrick Harbour station was a white elephant from the start. It was closed in 1868 - the very same year it was opened!

The Portpatrick Railway – later nicknamed 'The Paddy' – entered Wigtownshire at Newton Stewart and progressed across the moors to Stranraer and Portpatrick, with stations at Kirkcowan, Glenluce, Dunragit and Castle Kennedy. Viaducts were built to cross the River Bladnoch, Tarff Water and the Water of Luce. Between Stranraer and Portpatrick there was a stop at Colfin near Lochans.

Communities in the south of the county then began clamouring for rail links of their own. Plans for an extension into the south Rhins as far as Drummore were stillborn. But the Wigtownshire Railway down the Machars peninsula went ahead. The first section, between Newton Stewart and Wigtown, was opened in 1875. The next section – taking in Kirkinner, Whauphill and Sorbie - was problematical. Garlieston needed to be served but the Earl of Galloway, despite being among the sponsors of the enterprise, did not want it spoiling the view from his Galloway House mansion. Garlieston's station was therefore to be at Millisle, a not insubstantial distance to the west. But almost as soon as this was completed in 1876, it was realised what a folly it had been, so the developers added a little branch from Millisle into Garlieston proper. Meanwhile the track-laying continued south and the terminus at Whithorn was reached in 1877. This final section had a tiny midway halt at Broughton Skeog but that was an early casualty of rationalisation.

The Wigtownshire Railway came to be affectionately nicknamed the 'Bullet', presumably because – if the following contemporary account is to be believed – it was nothing of the sort:

> It is one of those pleasant, unhurried, single-rail lines, where the same engines and carriages go backward and forward so many times a day, and the train moves along, at such a loitering pace, among the trim little stations that we have plenty of time to note and admire the scenery.

Donald MacIntosh's *Travels in Galloway* evokes fond memories of the line:

> The Machars Bullet may not have been the fastest train in Scotland, but there was no doubt that it was a pretty reliable old thing. The occasional snowdrift blocking a cutting might hold up its progress for an hour or two on winter evenings, and twice I remember sheep refusing to get off the track near to Whauphill. But it took more than leaves on the line or the wrong sort of snowflakes to block its progress. There was nothing namby-pamby about it. Like the Gallovidians who travelled on it, it was rugged and it took a lot to stop it...Your greatest danger on the Bullet...was in being blinded by flying cinders from the engine's smoke stack when you had the window open, or in having your legs and private parts welded to the seat by the occasional geyser of steam erupting from the radiators situated underneath you.

The Machars line was closed in 1950. Portpatrick station was taken out of service in the same year, though the branch from Stranraer was kept open as far as Colfin to serve the creamery there. The 'Paddy' survived until 1965, finally felled by the infamous 'Beeching Axe'. Stranraer still has a rail connection, but northwards into Ayrshire, not across Galloway to Dumfries and the Border.

During the Second World War a new branch-line was created: the Cairnryan Military Railway (see Wartime Wigtownshire).

The coming of the railways opened up this far corner of Scotland to the Victorian and Edwardian tourist, and ever since then the **tourism** trade has steadily increased as a proportion of the county's annual turnover. The business of catering for the leisure-time of the townee has to a large extent compensated for the employment shortfall created by the post-war mechanisation of agriculture.

For Wigtownshire tourism has not been the environmental disaster that it has proved to be for some other rural parts of the British Isles. The typical Shire holidaymaker is a seeker after beauty, wisdom and wholesomeness. The green-fingered rejoice in the exotic Gulf Stream splendour of the Logan, Castle Kennedy and Glenwhan gardens (see Part 1 – Port Logan/Castle Kennedy/ Dunragit). History enthusiasts pore over the abundant heritage of archaeological sites, most notably at Whithorn's 'cradle of Christianity' (see The Early History). Bibliophiles flock to Scotland's official Book Town at Wigtown. Fans of the cult movie *The Wicker Man* follow the trail of its bonnie locations throughout the county (see The Movies). Ornithologists find the Wigtownshire coastline to be a bird-watching paradise.

For walkers of the hardier variety there is the attraction of the **Southern Upland Way**. This coast-to-coast path across the south of Scotland begins, or alternatively ends, in Wigtownshire. Setting off from here and walking eastwards is the official recommendation: doing it in that direction means that the wind, rain and sun are largely at one's back.

The starting-point is Portpatrick. The path proceeds northwards along the coast to Killantringan Lighthouse and then takes a north-easterly direction towards Stranraer but avoids the town by heading east towards Castle Kennedy. After passing through Castle Kennedy Gardens it meanders across the moors and through the forests of the often bleak northern part of the county until finally leaving Wigtownshire at Bargrennan. The whole route from Portpatrick to Cockburnspath on the Berwickshire coast is 212 miles long; depending on the level of fitness and the degree of determination, it can take between ten and twenty days to complete.

Nowadays not all of the outsiders coming to the Shire are just passing through as holidaymakers. More and more are staying put as **new settlers**, not only retirees but also working people seeking an alternative to the stresses of overcrowding elsewhere. This immigration, combined with the unceasing demand among the urban professional classes for second homes, has inflated property prices beyond the buying capacity of the locals who provide the essential basic services. The 'white settlers', as they are often referred to, are overwhelmingly from south of the Border and the scale of the influx is such as to have reduced the old Scots tongue of the Shire almost to a minority position. During the first millennium AD, the Angles colonised the area but eventually withdrew (see The Early History). Now in the third millennium, it seems, their descendents are returning to finish the job off.

The Irish Connection

First-time visitors to Wigtownshire, travelling southwards from Ayrshire or westwards from Kirkcudbrightshire, soon start to detect a distinctively different tone to the local Scots speech. The **accent** has an unmistakably Irish tinge. Close your eyes, eavesdrop on the talk of the street and you could well imagine yourself to be in Ulster (though these days you may for this exercise have to filter out the almost equally pervasive sound coming from the new wave of English settlers). In 1818 the English poet John Keats, not an incomer but just passing through during a walking-tour (see Other Pairs of Eyes), noticed the similarity. Having visited both sides of the North Channel through making a return journey between Portpatrick and Donaghadee, he came to the conclusion that 'the dialect on the neighbouring shores of Scotland and Ireland is much the same'.

In large part this remains true to this day, not only in the similarity of inflection but also in a common **vocabulary**, eg *bairn* [child], *bogle* [supernatural spirit], *burn* [stream], *fankle* [become tangled], *fash* [worry, as in *dinnae fash yersel*, 'don't get upset'], *flit* [move house], *girn* [complain], *greet* [cry], *lassie* [girl], *peely-wally* [pale or sickly] and *skelf* [splinter]. The bond of speech is symbolised by the Scots word used on both sides as a colloquialism for the North Channel itself: the *Sheuch* [ditch].

A humorous story from Northern Ireland demonstrates the linguistic links between Wigtownshire and Ulster. A man from Ballymena in Antrim had English neighbours who produced a son. 'Whit are ye gaun tae cry [call] him?' inquired the Ulsterman in the purest Scots. 'We're thinking of calling him Nathan,' replied the Englishman. 'Och, ye'll hae tae cry him *somethin*!' [for those unfamiliar with the language it should be explained that the sound of 'Nathan' is almost identical to that of Scots *naethin*, 'nothing'].

That story is told in *The Scottish World*, 'a journey into the Scottish diaspora' by Billy Kay, a leading present-day populariser of the Scots language, who is native to Wigtownshire's northern neighbour Ayrshire. His personal account of discovering Ulster Scots could have been the experience of anyone from either county:

> I had a friend in the English Language course at Edinburgh University called Linde Connolly...who hailed from the Bushmills area of Co. Antrim. As a course assignment, we had to write an essay on our local

> dialects. Before handing the essays in, we decided to have a look at each other's work, thinking they would be completely different. As we had only ever spoken Standard English to one another, I was quite taken aback to discover that Linde and I spoke almost exactly the same dialect – the west central dialect of Scots – differing only slightly in Ayrshire and Antrim inflections.

Vivid testimony to the continuity of this cross-channel kinship of tongue came during the 2007 Wigtown Book Festival when the opening address was given – nay, hollered – by the Rev Ian Paisley, the Presbyterian demagogue who famously made peace with his Sinn Fein enemies and became the inaugural First Minister of Northern Ireland. The sound of his stentorian Antrim voice booming across the town square did not seem at all out of place. The same festival had an event which was billed as 'Galloway Irish Meets Ulster Scots' and was described as follows: 'the comic poems of Wigtownshire's Ian McHarg are matched with the songs of Antrim's Willie Drennan in this light-hearted celebration...The event takes place on the Stena HSS fast ferry between Belfast and Stranraer, the perfect location to re-unite these estranged linguistic cousins'.

Given the **geographical closeness** of the two coastlines, it is hardly surprising that from the beginning of recorded history there has been a continuous interchange of peoples, ideas and modes of speech. Legend has it that in one miraculous giant step **St Patrick** leapt across the Sheuch from where Portpatrick now is, to begin his mission to Ireland. His footprint is supposed to be buried beneath the foundations of the dock development that was meant (but in the end failed) to make Portpatrick rich through exploiting the fact that it is only some twenty-one miles from Donaghadee, its maritime counterpart on the Ards peninsula of County Down. This nautical connection is often loosely described as the shortest sea-crossing between Scotland and Ireland. To be more precise, it is the shortest between Wigtownshire and Ireland. If you were an Irish crow looking for the straight line across to Scotland, you would be well advised to fly from Fair Head on the north-east coast of Antrim to the Mull of Kintyre in Argyll. As the crow flies, that is a good eight miles shorter.

On the subject of St Patrick, there is an alternative version of his crossing the Sheuch. It is said that on his way to the Rhins he got into a spot of bother, the result of which was that he was beheaded. Undaunted, the intrepid missionary picked himself up (literally) and pressed on for the western seaboard. Unable to find a boat to take him across, he swam instead, his shorn-off head clenched between his teeth!

Of course, as far as Scots are concerned, the most important fact about Ireland is that that is where they came from in the first place. Had there not been steady migration of the ***Scotti*** [Latin] from Ireland from the sixth century onwards, there would not have been a Scotland, or certainly not the country as we know it (it would probably have been Pictland!). As every Scottish schoolboy/girl knows (or used to know before proper education went out of fashion around 1965), these northbound Irish immigrants settled principally in modern Argyll, forming the small kingdom of Dalriada or Dal Riata, the nucleus of the larger united Scotland which emerged by the ninth century.

Of these early emigrants from the Emerald Isle, not all made it as far north as Argyll. Faced with the dangers and uncertainties of the long voyage up through Hebridean waters, how tempting it must have been to opt instead for the first stretch of land to come into sight. Alternatively, how easy it must have been for their small wicker-and-hide boats or coracles [Irish Gaelic *curragh*] to have been blown off-course towards the east. Whatever the reason, intention or accident, some of these Hibernian wanderers landed in what is now Wigtownshire, and the undulating fertile territory was sufficiently inviting for them to settle. A sixth-century chronicler described 'foul crowds' of them emerging 'like dark hordes of maggots from the narrowest cracks and recesses when the sun is overhead and its rays grow warm.' Confirmation of the scattered presence of Gaelic-speaking Irish *Scotti* here from the 400s (and possibly even earlier) has come from the recent detective work of place-name scholars.

Place-names throughout the county testify specifically to the strong influence of early **Irish Christianity**. The original Irish migrants were converts to the cult of Christ, and when the new faith took hold over the native Brittonic population through the missionary work ascribed to St Ninian (see The Early History), there was a continuous exchange of clerical personnel between Whithorn and its sibling communities across the water. It was overwhelmingly the saints of Ireland who were commemorated in so many of the county's ancient ecclesiastical settlements, such as Chapel Finian (see Part 1 – Port William) and the numerous sites on either side of Luce Bay that are traditionally associated with St

Medan (see Part 1 – Kirkmaiden/ Monreith).

The story of all the subsequent waves of immigrants who came to compete with the aboriginal Britons and the new-arrival Irish for a share in the lands of the northern Solway region has been told in the previous chapter. The point here is that once the kingdom of Rheged had contracted back to Cumbria and the Angles had retreated home to Northumbria and the Vikings had taken the return trip to Scandanavia, the **Gall Gaidheil** culture that remained rooted here was Gaelic-speaking and still closely aligned to its Irish origins. We get a flavour of this cross-channel commonwealth through the enigmatic figure, emerging fleetingly from the mists of Dark Ages history, of one Echmarcach mac Ragnaill. When he died during a pilgrimage to Rome in 1065, this Irish Sea chieftain was 'king' of the Rhins. But – and here is the significant bit – he had also for a time been king of Dublin. Perhaps we may think in terms of a Dublin-Drummore axis!

The post-Echmarcach leadership that emerged, more recognisably to us, and that ruled for most of the next two centuries was that of the Lords of Galloway, from Fergus through Uchtred, Gilbert and Roland to Alan (see The Early History). Diplomatically, while they maintained arm's-length links with the kingdom of Scotland to their north, their natural gravitation was towards the south and the west in and around the Irish Sea. Their naval capability in the region was prodigious. In return for military service on behalf of King John of England, Alan received gifts of land in Ireland. When he was widowed and still without a legitimate male heir, he sought a new wife and found her in Ireland. Alan's warrior brother Thomas was gifted the castle at Coleraine and he too married an Irish woman, becoming, through her, the earl of Atholl. From Irish Gaelic *Diorbhorguil* Alan named his beloved youngest daughter Dervorguilla, she of Sweetheart Abbey fame (see *The Kirkcudbrightshire Companion*).

For the sea-faring lords of Galloway Loch Ryan was a magnificently convenient terminal for the **military route to Ireland**, as it was for the later kings of Scotland. The Sheuch link was vital in a great military adventure of 1317. By this time the lordship of Galloway had been absorbed into greater Scotland (on Alan's death in 1234) and the Ayrshire warlord Robert Bruce had become indisputably King after defeating the English occupiers of Scotland at the Battle of Bannockburn. Three years after this turning-point victory, King Robert, at the head of a naval expeditionary force, set sail from Loch Ryan and landed at Larne on the Antrim coast.

He crossed over in support of his younger brother Edward who was already there with an army trying to seize English-held territory.

For Robert it was the opening up of a new front against England, while Edward, not content with the title Lord of Galloway which his brother had revived for him, was aspiring to his own kingship, that of Ireland. Some of the Gaelic chiefs did nominate him as 'High King of Ireland' but his ambition came to nothing. After an unsuccessful military campaign almost the length and breadth of Ireland, Robert returned to Loch Ryan, along with many of the casualties, to attend to more pressing problems at home. Edward stayed on but in 1318 was killed near Dundalk. His body was decapitated, the head preserved in a bucket of salt and delivered as a triumphalist gift to Edward II of England.

The interesting aspect of King Robert's involvement in the Irish campaign is his stated belief in the continuing common tradition bridging the twenty or so miles of sea between Galloway and Ireland. Before setting off he had written to the Irish chiefs about recovering the ancient liberty of *nostra nacio* [Latin, 'our people'], a phrase asserting that Ireland and Irish-founded Scotland were still to a large extent one big happy family of Celtic nations. The Irish chiefs for their part, in a letter to the Pope (who was attempting to broker an Anglo-Scottish reconciliation), wrote of the direct bloodline between greater Scotia (Ireland) and lesser Scotia (Scotland), the latter being described as keeping 'our language and way of life to a certain extent'.

Aside from mass movements of the Irish across the Sheuch – from the early settlers to the economic migrants of the later poverty-driven diaspora (see below) - the proximity of the two lands was a continuous opportunity for individual adventurism. The **Adair** or Adare clan took root in Wigtownshire around 1400 when, it is said, Robert Fitzgerald, son of the Earl of Desmond, sought refuge here to escape the consequences of a feud. He changed his name to Adair, taking it from land he had owned in the south of Ireland, and he and his descendents prospered in Wigtownshire to such an extent that in the rogues' gallery of medieval power-games the Adairs rank alongside the Agnews, the Maxwells, the McDoualls and the Kennedys.

Their original stronghold was Dunskey Castle, south of Portpatrick. Fitzgerald/Adair is said to have acquired it as a reward from the then King of Scotland for capturing and killing its unruly previous occupant. In time the Adair name became attached to territory throughout the county, the principal being the estate of

Kinhilt. It was Ninian Adair of Kinhilt who built the Castle of St John in Stranraer.

Then, in a striking reversal of the Adairs' story, after a couple of centuries they went back to Ireland, this time to the north. Having arrived in Scotland Catholics, they returned Presbyterians in the government-backed programme of settlement known as the **Plantations**, which were aimed at counteracting the 'disloyalty' of the old Gaelic culture. William Adair of Kinhilt acquired an estate that grew into the modern town of Ballymena in Antrim, though at first he tried calling it Kinhilstown. In a further twist of irony, the Adair lands around Dunskey, including Portree (later Portpatrick), passed into the hands of an Ayrshire laird who pioneered the whole idea of the Ulster plantation.

That laird was **Sir Hugh Montgomery** (1560-1636) of Braidstane near Beith. It was he who first developed the trading route between Portpatrick and Donaghadee, receiving from King James VI and I exclusive rights over cross-channel traffic. From 1606 he managed the emigration via Portpatrick of some 10,000 Scots, mainly to the Ards peninsula east of Belfast. The land on which they settled was in a poor state owing to war and neglect but, thanks to a lot of hard work and the good fortune of a couple of excellent harvests, the Scots transformed it. The town of Newtonards sprang up and by 1613 had won borough status. The new settlers were so successful that their example was the template for King James's own official plantations, to Virginia (1607), to the rest of Ulster (1610) and to Nova Scotia (1621). In gratitude the King elevated Montgomery to Viscount of the Great Ardes.

Montgomery sought immortality for his name by attempting to change Donaghadee to 'Montgomery' and Portpatrick to 'Port Montgomery'. He was denied that particular form of perpetuity but, four centuries on, he and his fellow countryman James Hamilton (a friend who became a rival) are now fully recognised and honoured as the 'Founding Fathers of the Ulster-Scots'.

Late in life, after the death of his first wife, Montgomery consolidated his links with Wigtownshire by marrying Sarah Maxwell, Countess of Wigtown. Sarah moved to Newtonards to be with her husband but within months she had returned home. The Scoto-Irish bonds of friendship were all very well – but who could have blamed her for missing the Shire?!

Some thirty years later many of these settlers were scurrying back across the Sheuch for safety following the outbreak in 1641 of the **Irish Rebellion**. The Catholic insurgents feared further restrictions on their religious liberty from the Puritan lobby that by now was dominating the English parliament. But it was not just the English planters but the Scots too who were targeted in the revolt. Fortunately for the Scottish incomers, the army of the Covenanters, fresh from victory in the Bishops' Wars against King Charles I, was available to come to their rescue. 4000 fighters landed at Carrickfergus and before long the Scots' army of liberation had grown to 10,000-strong. They seized control of north-east Ulster, heartland of the Scots settlers. But by 1646 their luck had run out and they were thrashed by the Irish confederates at the battle of Benburb in Co Armagh. Loch Ryan, which had seen over the centuries so many Ireland-bound military embarkations, once again welcomed back the casualties.

Meanwhile the threat from the native Irish gradually receded and the refugees on the Rhins could eventually return to their Ulster lands. Many more new recruits joined them during the rest of the seventeenth century. They included another Wigtownshire Adair to make his name across the channel: the Rev Patrick Adair (1624?-1693/4), remembered to this day as the first historian of Ulster Presbyterianism. Two centuries later the descendents of these emigrants would be the 'no surrender' Protestants of Ulster unionism pitted against the Catholics of Irish republicanism in the long, bitter 'Troubles' of the late twentieth century.

The **ferry service** between Wigtownshire and Ireland, still a vital link between the two countries, effectively began with Sir Hugh Montgomery's promotion of Portpatrick in the early years of the seventeenth century (see above). For another two centuries Portpatrick continued as the principal harbour for this purpose until its disadvantages became all too apparent and the cross-channel traffic was transferred to the less weather-exposed waters of Loch Ryan.

The switch to Stranraer might have taken place much sooner if successive governments had not been so obsessed with trying to exploit the narrowness of the sea gap between Portpatrick and Donaghadee for the transportation of both mail and military personnel. To this end the overland approach to Portpatrick was upgraded in the 1760s. This highway is still traceable on modern maps as the 'Old Military Road'. The original survey of the route stated that 'the intention of the proposed road is speedy and certain communication between Great Britain and Ireland, especially with regard to the passage of troops from one Kingdom to another'. A century later the railway developers in Galloway were actively encouraged to make Portpatrick their seaward terminus, though almost at once Stranraer replaced it as the maritime gateway for the county (see Part 1 – Portpatrick).

The early ferries from Portpatrick were nothing like today's sleek floating palaces of pleasure plying between Stranraer-Cairnryan and Belfast-Larne. The onboard space was shared by man and beast. For a long time there were no proper berthing facilities. On the approach to Portpatrick passengers had to be transferred to smaller craft for landing, while the cattle and horses were shoved overboard and forced to swim ashore.

Numerous distinguished travellers of the eighteenth century have left vivid testimony of the difficulties they encountered. In October 1747 Richard Pococke, an English clergyman with an Irish bishopric, who wrote classic accounts of his extensive travels, was trying to reach his adopted homeland and noted:

> Sent my things aboard, but being windy would not go, they had a terrible wet passage...We sailed [the next day] in 5 hours to Donaghadee, a fine passage but I was very sick; - they go in open Hoys [small coasting vessels], which have no deck. I took over my excellent mare.

Pococke was again making the crossing in 1760, this time in the opposite direction, and was not impressed by the scene on the Scottish side:

> ...early in the morning, I arrived at Port Patrick in Scotland, which is a very poor place. Here they ship the horses from a rock, and when they land them from Ireland they help them out of the packet-boat into the sea, when they have brought the boat as near as they can to the shore.

In 1765 the Methodist evangelist John Wesley was heading for Ireland but, on reaching Portpatrick, discovered that the wind was 'full in our teeth' and decided to delay his trip until the following day. He wrote in his diary: 'It seemed strange to cross the sea in an open boat, especially when the winds ran high. I was a little sick, till I fell asleep. In five hours and a half we reached Donaghadee.'

James Boswell, famous biographer of Dr Samuel Johnson, was off on one of his amorous adventures in 1769 when he 'engaged' a boat at Portpatrick (there was no timetabled service in those days, just a kind of maritime taxi-rank). He was heading for Mary Ann in Dublin, his *belle irlandaise* who was just sixteen but 'formed like a Grecian nymph…her little bosom beats at thoughts of seeing me' (adding, however, 'forgive my vanity'). But Boswell's own not-so-little bosom was beating at the prospect of a choppy crossing:

> As we knew we would be sick, we determined to sail that night and try to sleep, as there was a good cabin...At twelve my companion and I went aboard. I tried to brave it out for a while, but grew very sick. She was better than I. Only I got some sleep, which she did not. Nothing can be severer than to be sick at sea, for one has no hope that immediate relief may come, as in other sicknesses. One grows quite weak. I thought my Irish jaunt madness, and that I would not try another.

[He did not need to 'try another': when he got to Dublin he discovered that his ardour for Mary Ann had abated!]

The first Stranraer ferries became in effect extensions of the new railway network. The railway companies required more predictability compared with the previous vagaries of the operation. There was therefore a move towards railway acquisition of the shipping. The first fully timetabled service between Stranraer and Larne began in 1872.

In the early years of the twentieth century the principal craft were all Princesses: *Margaret*, *Maud* and *Victoria*. According to Laurence Liddle, author of *Passenger Ships of the Irish Sea 1919-1969*, *Margaret* and *Maud* were notorious 'rollers':

> For saloon passengers, excellent breakfasts and evening meals were available but, on occasions, weather conditions in the North Channel...precluded their consumption, at least in any degree of comfort. I have a vivid recollection of one such occasion [1938]...The weather was such that the degree of acrobatic expertise needed to consume breakfast was rather greater than a landsman, such as myself, possessed.

The concept of royal females continued after the Second World War: the *Ailsa Princess*, the *Antrim Princess*, the *Caledonian Princess* (later turned into a Tyneside floating night-club called the *Tuxedo Princess*!) and the *Galloway Princess*.

Over the years their ownership and their routes changed at a bewildering rate. After the separate regional railway companies were nationalised in 1948, the new state-owned British Railways operated the Stranraer-Larne link, connecting with the 'Paddy' train to and from London. In 1969 BR's maritime division took the name 'Sealink' but that eventually disappeared following the denationalisation of the 1980s, to be replaced by the names of successive new owners. Sea Containers took over in 1984, followed in 1990 by Stena. Meanwhile, a rival service from Cairnryan was started by Townsend Thorenson who were then replaced by P & O. In 1995 Stena switched Stranraer's Irish destination from Larne to Belfast. Ship names have now lost much of their romantic resonance. *Stena Voyager* and *P & O Express* are dully non-specific by comparison, while *European Highlander* is a blatant misnomer in the North Channel.

There is one ship name that still sends shivers down the spine at the memory of its tragic ending in 1953: the ***Princess Victoria***. There have in fact been four vessels of that name and there would seem to have been something of a jinx upon the title, for two of them met disaster. *Princess Victoria* III was introduced to the Stranraer-Larne route in 1939 as the first drive-on, drive-off car ferry. But, like so many of the civilian ships of the Irish sea, it was soon commandeered into the war effort as a minelayer. She had been doing duty along the Baltic and North Sea coasts for only months when she fell foul of a German mine in the Humber estuary. Forty-four of her crew perished.

The loss of the *Princess Victoria* IV was even more catastrophic and it was not the result of enemy action. Her sinking on January 31 1953, killing 133 people, was Britain's worst-ever peacetime maritime disaster. There were only 44 survivors.

The weather was certainly stormy that Saturday morning but Captain James Ferguson had no reason to believe that the conditions were much out of the ordinary. He discovered otherwise as the ship left Loch Ryan and entered the open sea. One and a quarter hours after leaving Stranraer, the stern doors to the car deck were smashed open by a giant wave and the crew could not get them closed again. With ferocious speed the car deck was flooded and the ship lurched sideways.

The first of sixty Morse Code messages was sent by wireless operator David Broadfoot: 'Hove to off mouth of Loch Ryan. Vessel not under command. Urgent assistance of tug required.' But there were no tugs available. Because of poor visibility the crew were not entirely sure of their whereabouts so, when the Portpatrick lifeboat set out, the directions they had been given were inaccurate. HMS Contest, which had been despatched from Rothesay, came tantalisingly close but was also hampered by the low visibility. The last message from the *Princess Victoria* was received at 1.58pm.

One of the ship's lifeboats, containing most of the women and children, smashed against the sinking hull and sank. Not a single woman or child survived. The lucky ones were picked up by the lifeboat from Donaghadee in County Down. Neither Broadfoot nor Fergusson made any attempt to save himself: the wireless operator stayed at his post, while the captain was last seen on the bridge raising a salute. The dead included Maynard Sinclair, deputy prime minister of Northern Ireland. A subsequent inquiry concluded that the stern doors had not been sturdy enough.

Though there have never again been mishaps on the scale of the *Princess Victoria* sinking, the *Antrim Princess* came close to disaster in the winter of 1983. Its engine-room caught fire shortly after leaving Larne and the ship, having lost power, drifted to within a quarter of a mile of the Antrim coast. 128 passengers were mightily relieved to be airlifted from the stricken vessel by RAF helicopters.

When it was still the main ferry terminal Portpatrick had for almost a century a reputation as the **'Gretna Green for Ireland'**. In 1753 so-called 'clandestine' marriages were outlawed in England and Ireland. The only alternative then for 'runaway' couples was Scotland, where marriage 'by declaration' before witnesses in a place other than a church remained legal. English couples could slip over the Border to Gretna Green and to Annan in Dumfriesshire. For the Irish a quick trip across the Sheuch was the more practicable option.

Portpatrick was able to mount a marital service that went well beyond what the blacksmith's anvils of Dumfriesshire were offering. It could sell the charade of a Christian ceremony, thanks to the unorthodox participation of the local kirk ministry. While the lay registrars of Gretna and Annan were transparently secular, successive ministers at Portpatrick provided a veneer of religious respectability by bending the Church of Scotland rules. There was an official requirement for the couple to have had a minimum period of residence in the parish, and this was to be attested to by the reading of the banns three times on the Sabbath before a congregation. In Portpatrick this stipulation was compacted into three readings of the banns on the *same* Sabbath, sometimes in an empty kirk.

Though strangers to the parish, the couple had no shortage of potential witnesses. That was all part of the package, the minister calling on the services of the proprietor of the couple's lodgings or the captain of the boat on which they had arrived or even the minister's own relatives. The minimum fee was £10, a substantial amount at that time. Whereas the ministers who sometimes cooperated in the Annan marriage trade donated their fees to the poor, in Portpatrick the money went straight into the clerical pocket.

A survey of the parish records between 1759 and 1826 revealed that 234 ‘irregular’ marriages took place. Because of the expense involved a Portpatrick ‘irregular’ was usually not a possibility for the less affluent. A high proportion of the ceremonies were for members of the Irish gentry. This scandalous marriage trade was finally ended in 1826, though only after it had been publicly denounced by sections of the clergy who were not profiting from it.

Over a thousand years after the original Irish settlers arrived in Wigtownshire, immigration from the same source but of a very different kind had a profound effect on the social and economic life of the county. From the second half of the eighteenth century onwards the poverty-driven **Irish diaspora** began in earnest and for many of those who decided to try their luck in Scotland the Shire was a temptingly convenient destination.

The scale of the inflow was soon a matter of public debate and much resentment against the incomers was stirred up. An official report in the 1790s claimed that Stranraer 'is oppressed with Irish vagrants, who come over in crowds'. It was claimed that a single newspaper advertisement for labour ‘will bring over hundreds of them in a few days’.

The situation was complicated during the closing years of the century by the repercussions of the conflict between the Protestant authorities in Dublin and the United Irishmen who were agitating for Catholic emancipation. A government crackdown on the activists led many of them to seek refuge in Wigtownshire. Popular distrust of them presumably underlies the Rhins folk-tale about the fairy that dances gleefully every time a refugee is found shot dead. In *Tales of Galloway* (1979) Alan Temperley re-tells this story under the title ‘The Fairy Who Hated the Irish’.

The flow of immigrants into the county continued throughout the nineteenth century, with particularly large influxes in the aftermath of the potato famine of the 1840s and during the railway boom of the 1860s and ’70s. Stranraer had a ghetto known as Little Ireland. Accounts of their presence in communities throughout the area usually centred on their ‘wretchedness’. In the 1840s one kirk minister complained they were 'mostly of the lower orders of the Irish', while another wrote that ‘their habitations are too frequently the scenes of filth’. No doubt the ministers’ major grouse, though not stated publicly, was that they were overwhelmingly Roman Catholic, in other words customers of the ecclesiastical opposition.

Another frequent complaint was that their availability for low-paid work depressed the wages for the native population. A local newspaper commentary in 1845 stated:

> There are plenty of Irishmen ready to take the bread out of the mouths of our own poor. An Irishman who lives in a hovel, feeds on potatoes and neither clothes nor educates his children, can always work for less than a Scot. There are too many people who employ only the cheapest workers and do not think of the consequences.

So many passed across the North Channel that the rocky island Ailsa Craig, clearly visible on the approach to Loch Ryan, was nicknamed Paddy's Milestone. Virtually every parish reported a sense of being swamped. In Whithorn, for example, the scale of settlement was described in the 1840s by the kirk minister as 'almost incredible'. The editors of the *New Statistical Account* (1845) estimated that fifteen per cent of the county's population were either Irish-born or of Irish parentage.

The Irish penetration of Wigtownshire society is comically described in Robert Trotter's *Galloway Gossip* (1877):

> Now you could scarcely find a real Scotch cotman or drainer in the county; the very herds in the muirs are often half Irish, and a large proportion of the tradesmen as well...Wigtonshire, if named after its inhabitants, might now justly be called Little Ulster, or New Belfast...or something of that kind.

Trotter calls them 'patlanders', and he describes a supposed ethnic divide across the Rhins between the Norse-descended 'Fingauls' in the south and the Irish-descended 'Gossoks' in the north ('I might give some of their family names, but as the description of their looks is not very flattering, I will not give needless offence'!).

Trotter pokes fun at their propensity for de-Irish-ing their surnames, a phenomenon which he describes as a social disease 'very much resembling Gentility'. He cites an example:

> Twa men frae Ireland cam ower to make drains for Col. Andrew McDouall of Logan, for he was a horrid man for improvements, and had hundreds of Irishmen drainin till him. Yin o' the twa they ca't O'Toole, an' the ither O'Dowd, and they both married and settled in the Rhinns, an' their sons became Mr Doyle and Mr Doud. The grandchildren now call themselves McDouall and Dodds.

He gives other examples of name-changing: from 'O'Carrol' to

'Charles', from 'O'Forgan' to 'Ferguson' and from 'O'Corcoran' to 'Cochrane'. 'And so on', he concludes, 'till you would think no Irishman had ever settled in Galloway'.

Seasonal Irish workers were still coming in large numbers for the Shire tattie harvests until the 1940s and the tradition did not entirely disappear until the 1980s. But in more recent years another form of Irish penetration has been taking place but this time wealth rather than poverty has been the driving-force. The so-called **Celtic Tiger**, the name given to the EU-sponsored economic turnaround in the Irish economy, has created substantial surpluses of cash in agriculture on the other side of the Sheuch, and much of this capital has been invested in the purchase of Wigtownshire farmland. Long-established local farmers no longer consider it to be worth the stress to serve the rapacious supermarket leviathan. For farmers from Ireland, where land can cost twice as much, this native exodus from the business has presented plenty of opportunities. In 2006 a Galloway land agent commented: 'We have seen a steady migration over the years but in the last year it has turned into a flood.'

It has been by sea that this hugely varied inter-reaction between two coastlines has been taking place during the past couple of millennia (at least). But now we are presented with an enticing vision of a new kind of passage between Portpatrick and Donaghadee for the twenty-first century and beyond. In 2007 an Irish think-tank published proposals for an underwater **railway tunnel** and the idea appears to be gathering momentum, though implementation, if it ever comes about, is a long, long way off. The Rev Ian Paisley, during that visit to Wigtown mentioned above, had his own characteristically robust way of endorsing the proposal. 'They did it with those frog-eaters of France', he said, 'and so our porridge-eaters in Northern Ireland should be entitled to it as well!'

The idea of a tunnel (or possibly even a bridge) will be scrutinised carefully by local authorities and businesses on both sides of the Sheuch. They now have an official forum for the discussion of such matters of common interest. It is called the North Channel Partnership.

The 'North Channel Partnership': not a bad phrase for two thousand years of across-the-water Celtic bonding!

Wartime Wigtownshire

Though far removed from the twentieth-century theatres of conflict, Wigtownshire nonetheless made a major contribution of its own to the UK's military preparedness. Precisely because it was peripheral, the county was the ideal location for training personnel and trying out weaponry. The British defence establishment took full advantage during the Second World War and before long there was hardly any part of the Shire that was not in close proximity to military facilities.

The county's connection with the military had begun, in a modest way, during the First World War when **East Freugh**, due south from Castle Kennedy, was used from 1915 as a base for airships patrolling the Irish Sea and North Channel. Their purpose was to spot German submarines. They were not adept at hitting the target but were useful for passing on sightings to anti-submarine vessels on the surface.

In the run-up to the Second World War the government acquired 2,600 acres at **West Freugh**. At first this was an armament training camp. Later in the war it diversified into the honing of air navigation and bomb-aiming skills. Practice targets were set up in Luce Bay and on nearby moorland.

RAF Wigtown, also specialising in air observer training, was established at Baldoon near Bladnoch. While the airfield was being built in 1941 the workers were entertained by the legendary Gracie Fields. After it became operational the iconic Scottish music-hall entertainer Sir Harry Lauder came to give a concert.

There were many less happy occasions at Baldoon. Of the aircraft that took off on training missions from RAF Wigtown between 1941 and 1945, twenty-seven never returned and sixty-seven people lost their lives. One theory is that pilots, frustrated by lack of real-life action, kept up their excitement by taking too many risks. Many of the casualties were buried in the kirkyard at Kirkinner.

An extraordinary target for aerial bombing exercises was set up on **Braid Fell** north-east of Stranraer. Here in 1941 a replica of an entire factory building typical of Hitler's industrial heartland of the Ruhr was constructed. The bombers in training must have targeted this one with particular relish.

In 1940, fearing devastating German bombing of Clydeside, the government went in search of suitable sites for emergency harbours. Two in Scotland were identified. Faslane on the Gareloch became Military Port No 1. Wigtownshire provided the other: **Cairnryan Military Port No 2**. By 1941 some four thousand people had converged on the area to begin the construction not only of two new deep-water piers but also of the **Cairnryan Military Railway**, a dedicated branch-line leaving the Dumfries-Stranraer main-line at Castle Kennedy. The work was completed by 1943. Before the wartime railway was officially opened it was used in 1942 by King George VI and Queen Elizabeth to reach Cairnryan from where they embarked on a visit to Northern Ireland.

The rest of Loch Ryan was also busy with military activity. The flying-boats of **RAF Stranraer** were stationed here throughout most of the Second World War. **RAF Wig Bay**, on the west side of the loch just down from Kirkcolm, was the flying-boats' maintenance depot. North of Kirkcolm, **RAF Corsewall**, based at Corsewall House, was a facility for training in the handling of marine craft.

Also in the north Rhins, **Lochnaw Castle** was taken over in 1940 as a military hospital. In 1942, when it was thought that the Americans were going to set up their own flying-boat facility on Loch Ryan, the castle hospital was offered to them. They insisted, however, on a new build within the castle grounds. But then the US plan for a base was abandoned and Britain took over completion of the American hospital, only to encounter problems with sourcing material that conformed to the original American specifications. Eventually the new building was completed and the hospital within the castle was de-commissioned.

At **Burrow Head** on the southern tip of the Machars peninsula there was an anti-aircraft gunnery practice camp. Various methods were employed to launch moving targets. Some were catapulted from Burrow Head. Others were towed by aircraft flying out of West Freugh. Then a dedicated airfield was created to the north-west at **Kidsdale** near Glasserton, from where radio-controlled Tiger Moth bi-planes, nicknamed 'Queen Bees', took off. **Castle Kennedy Airfield** was also used for air-gunnery exercises.

The south Rhins did not entirely miss out on the military action. An emergency landing-strip was constructed at **Low Eldrig** north of Drummore, while **Drummore** itself was host to an air-sea rescue unit.

In the final stages of the Second World War, Wigtownshire had a crucial role in preparations for the liberation of Europe from the grip of Nazi Germany through its involvement in the **Mulberry Harbour Project**. An Allied landing on the French coast had long been in the planning. Access to port facilities would be vital but the difficulty of capturing a French port had been made apparent in 1942 during the disastrous attempt on Dieppe. Churchill's solution was brilliant but simple: they would just have to take their own harbour with them.

Thus was born the project to create a floating harbour consisting of components that could be towed across the English Channel and assembled off the Normandy coast. The official specification was for 'a pierhead capable of berthing three 2000-ton vessels simultaneously and a pier which would allow continuous traffic flow over a length of not less than one mile'. The project's codename was Mulberry.

While the parts were to be manufactured at shipyards and engineering works throughout Britain, a single location was chosen for testing the three principal prototypes and that was the area around **Garlieston** on the west side of Wigtown Bay. The site included **Rigg Bay** to the south of the village and **Portyerrock Bay** near the Isle of Whithorn. Along this stretch of coast the beaches and tidal movements replicated those of Normandy and, being well out of the normal range of German aerial espionage, the area offered conditions of security. It was also advantageous that the people of Wigtownshire were already attuned to the war effort through hosting so many other military bases.

Royal Engineers began arriving in 1943. To accommodate them a camp was built at **Cairnhead** north of the Isle of Whithorn and Garlieston village hall was requisitioned. The following year, when training began for the troops who would assemble the Mulberries in the battle zone, **Glasserton House** was also taken over as barracks. Tempted by the contents of the wine-cellar at Glasserton, a number of soldiers, unable to pick the locks, dug through the kitchen floor. Their dipsomaniacal initiative led to their being court-martialled.

The Mulberry design that was eventually implemented was based on a series of concrete pontoons: 'Beetles' to take the roadway, and pierhead 'Spuds' with legs that rested on the seabed and adjusted themselves according to the tide. During late '43 and early '44 a frantic, flat-out national industrial effort went into the manufacture of twenty-two Spuds and ten miles of floating pier. Four pontoons were made at the **Cairn Point** fabrication facilities to the north of Cairnryan harbour.

One of the two other prototypes particularly intrigued Garliestonians. This was nicknamed the 'Swiss Roll', a length of temporary roadway that could be unrolled into a kind of 'magic carpet'. One morning, the 'Swiss Roll' having arrived in the harbour overnight, locals woke to find soldiers apparently walking on water.

By May of 1944 Garlieston was largely clear of the test materials, which had been transported to the south coast of England in readiness for the invasion. The Allied armada finally took off on D-Day, June 6, and the Mulberries followed immediately after. There were two of them: Mulberry A for the Americans, Mulberry B for the British. They were almost in place when on June 19 a storm damaged Mulberry A, as a result of which all supplies had to come in through Mulberry B. The British public were not told of this massive engineering project until late in the September, when an official announcement stated that 'two harbours each the size of Gibraltar Harbour have been built on the enemy coastline'. In no part of the UK was the news greeted more excitedly than in Garlieston.

Fifty years after the end of the war a granite memorial was erected in the village. The inscription leaves us in no doubt about Garlieston's role in 'thus making the INVASION OF EUROPE possible and an ALLIED VICTORY a reality'.

The existence of a flying-boat base in Loch Ryan proved to be useful during the war for high-level contact between the British and the Americans. In June 1942, for example, it was via Wigtownshire that Prime Minister **Winston Churchill** was able to visit the American president Franklin Roosevelt. A special train brought him from London to Cairnryan on the 17th. Then it was by motor-boat onto Loch Ryan where he and his entourage, including a personal doctor, boarded a Boeing Clipper flying-boat. General Sir Alan Brooke (later Viscount Alanbrooke) noted in his diary: 'Huge flying-boat, beautifully fitted up with bunks to sleep in, dining-saloon, steward's office, lavatories etc'. It took twenty-six and a half hours to cross the Atlantic. Brooke thought that the PM was 'enjoying himself like a schoolboy'. On the 27th, after several days of war-strategy meetings, Churchill arrived back at Cairnryan, where his special train was waiting to return him to London.

Wigtownshire was also one of the war-time meeting-places for Churchill and General (later President) Dwight Eisenhower. While planning the D-Day invasion of France, they held talks at **Knockinaam Lodge** overlooking Port of Spittal Bay south of Portpatrick. The lodge, a building of the mid-nineteenth century, was then still in the private ownership of the Hunter-Blair family. Now it is a dauntingly up-market hotel.

Naturally, the hotel management exploits this historic connection in its publicity (the 'Churchill' bedroom is in the highest price category). But at least two other hotels along the west coast of Scotland make similar claims in their marketing literature. The fact is that Churchill and Eisenhower, being respectively Britain's war leader and the Allied supreme commander in Europe, had countless meetings during 1943-44. Rather than specifically seeking out 'secret' locations, they met wherever was convenient for both of them at the time. There are no references to the Knockinaam get-together in any of the standard biographies of the two men.

Eisenhower wrote later of Churchill's mood-swings at their meetings and of his histrionic reaction whenever he was not getting his own way on a particular issue. This may well have been the scene at Knockinaam:

> He painted a terrible picture if we didn't do it...He said, 'If that should happen I should have to go to His Majesty and lay down the mantle of my high office'. And here are tears running down. But within seconds he was telling a joke.

Celebrities of the Shire

Sons of Wigtownshire (though disappointingly few of its daughters) have made many a mark on the public life of Britain at large - in politics, in the professions, and in academia and the arts.

Viscount Stair

Sir James Dalrymple, 1st Viscount Stair (1619-95) was not only a Wigtownshire laird but also a lawyer of national repute. He was the first legal luminary to attempt to codify Scots law. His *Institutions of the Law of Scotland* is still regarded as the foundation of modern practice. Today the organisation that exists to promote understanding of Scots law and of its history is called the Stair Society.

Dalrymple came originally from Ayrshire, where the family owned the Stair estate. His Wigtownshire connection was through marriage: his wife had substantial land-holdings around Glenluce. In 1674 he bought the Castle Kennedy estate, which remains in the hands of his descendents to this day (see Part 1 - Castle Kennedy).

He began his working life as an academic, staying on after graduation at Glasgow University to teach philosophy. Switching to law, he was called to the Bar in 1648 and became a judge in 1657.

A staunch Presbyterian and a supporter of the anti-Episcopalian National Covenant, in 1681 he resigned from the bench in protest against royal measures compromising the independence of the Church of Scotland. For a while he retired back to Wigtownshire. But, feeling threatened by the troops then persecuting Covenanters in the south-west, he took refuge in the Netherlands. While in exile he entered the circle of William of Orange who, along with his English royal wife Mary, would take on the British crown in the 'Glorious Revolution' that deposed the Catholic James VII & II. Dalrymple was aboard William and Mary's ship when they landed on the south coast of England in 1688. It was soon after this that the joint monarchs awarded him the viscountcy, for which he used the Stair appellation.

The newly installed regime also reinstated Stair as a judge in

Edinburgh. His record, however, is not without blemish. There was a parliamentary complaint of corruption against him and, although he was not found guilty, the courts were forced, as a result of the controversy surrounding Stair's methods, to make their decision-making processes more accountable.

Meanwhile, back in Wigtownshire, Stair's voracious acquisition of land and wealth appears to have been lubricated by his wily ways of doing business (see Part 1 - Dunragit). He died in Edinburgh and was buried there in the High Kirk of St Giles.

Four of his five sons followed him into the legal profession and all achieved high office (see below); the fifth son was a royal physician. The eldest of his five daughters became the stuff of legend through her ill-fated marriage to David Dunbar, heir to Baldoon Castle (see Part 1 - Bladnoch).

Stair's eldest son **John Dalrymple, 1st Earl of Stair** (1648-1707) became secretary of state for Scotland and gained a dubious place in the nation's history as the man primarily responsible for the notorious Massacre of Glencoe in 1692.

On the death of his father in 1695 Dalrymple junior succeeded to the viscountcy before his later elevation to an earldom. Like his father, he became a lawyer but most of his professional life was spent in government service. Personal scruples were never an obstacle to his gaining official position. Despite being Protestant and supportive of the Covenanters' cause, he ingratiated himself with the Catholic James VII & II and was appointed the King's Lord Advocate in Scotland. When the 'Glorious Revolution' of 1688 restored Protestant rule under William and Mary, Stair managed to get re-appointed. In the words of a twentieth-century historian, he was 'prepared to serve the new court as he had done the previous one as long as the rewards were forthcoming'. He went on to curry favour with a third royal regime, that of Queen Anne; it was she who made him an earl in 1704.

As for the business of Glencoe: there was much sympathy among the clans of the Highlands for the deposed monarch James Stuart. King William insisted, however, that the clan chiefs should all formally declare their loyalty, a policy which Dalrymple carried out with alacrity. When, owing to bad weather and a series of misunderstandings, MacIan, a Macdonald of Glencoe, failed to sign the oath by the official deadline, Stair gleefully seized the opportunity to make sure that the 'thieving tribe were rooted out'. On February 13, 1692 some forty of the clan were butchered by government soldiers; later there were more fatalities when those who had managed to escape perished in a snowstorm. A parliamentary committee of inquiry the following year blamed Stair above all. He stood down as secretary of state but the king formally absolved him of any responsibility for the massacre.

Stair was a strong supporter of the Union between Scotland and England, and he participated in the proceedings that led eventually to the abolition in 1707 of the original Scottish parliament. However, shortly before the Union was enacted, he died suddenly in his Edinburgh bed.

2nd Earl of Stair

As only the second son of the 1st Earl of Stair, John Dalrymple junior would not have succeeded to the title and become **2nd Earl of Stair** (1673-1747) had he not, at the age of eight, accidentally shot dead his elder brother. His parents were so disgusted by the incident that they sent young John away and, after three years residing with a tutor, he ended up being looked after by his grandfather, Viscount Stair (see above), who was then in political exile in the Netherlands. There the young Dalrymple met William of Orange and was another member of his family to be favoured for public appointments when William and Mary gained power in Britain in 1688-9.

For most of his career the 2nd Earl was a military commander and a diplomat. Like his father, he was virulently anti-Jacobite. When he was George I's ambassador in Paris he kept tabs on the exiled Stuart court there and was able to predict the Jacobite Rebellion of 1715. Again like his father, he was a powerful advocate of the Union and in 1707, when the Scottish parliament disbanded itself, he was among the first representative peers at the new parliament of Great Britain.

Away from public life, the 2nd Earl was one of the landowners behind the early-eighteenth-century turnaround in Wigtownshire's agriculture. In 1723 he was a founding member of the Society of Improvers in the Knowledge of Agriculture. On his own estates he was among the first to develop large-scale cultivation of turnips and cabbages.

His wife Eleanor was a formidable woman, famed for her good looks. Her traumatic experience of an earlier marriage, to Viscount Primrose, gave the writer Sir Walter Scott an idea for one of his *Chronicles of the Canongate* (1827). Primrose was a particularly nasty wife-beater. One day Eleanor saw in a window a reflection of him coming threateningly towards her with a sword in his hand. Half-naked, she escaped through the window and refused to go back to him. He eventually moved abroad.

Several months later she visited a fortune-teller. During the consultation he led her across to a mirror in which, according to the account she wrote later that day, she saw a vision of a wedding ceremony. The groom was none other than her husband and among the guests was one of her brothers. Some time later the brother returned home from a trip to the Netherlands. He told her of having been invited to the wedding of a friend's daughter, only to discover that the man standing at the altar was Viscount Primrose. The brother intervened and the marriage was halted. Eleanor retrieved the account of her earlier vision and discovered to everyone's amazement that it had happened on very day of her husband's thwarted bigamy.

Eleanor, after her estranged husband died in 1706, vowed that she would never marry again. However, the 2nd Earl pursued her relentlessly and eventually she agreed to become his Countess. Unfortunately, it looked at first as if she had entered another abusive marriage. The Earl was a heavy drinker and, under the influence, was sometimes violent towards her. One night he hit her in the face. The following morning he was overcome by remorse when he saw her weeping and covered in blood. He promised to mend his ways.

Eleanor's own favourite tipple was mineral water, which she often consumed from the well at Moffat in Dumfriesshire, thus helping to turn the place into a popular spa-resort. In Edinburgh, London and Bath she was well-known as a society hostess. Her name lives on in Edinburgh: her home off the Lawnmarket in the Royal Mile now houses the Writers' Museum but the building itself is still known as Lady Stair's House.

An odd thing happened with the 2nd Earl's succession. He and Eleanor had no children. The estates and the title were willed to one of his favourite nephews, yet another John Dalrymple, who duly inherited in 1747. But, while he retained the land, his tenure of the 3rd earldom came to an end the following year after a successful legal challenge by another nephew, who then became the 3rd Earl instead. The 3rd Earl's brother succeeded as the 4th Earl, and it was only on his death in 1768 that the man who had briefly been the 3rd became the 5th!

Sir John Ross

Sir John Ross (1777-1856), the celebrated Arctic explorer, was a Wigtownshire son of the manse, his father being the minister at Inch. By profession Ross was a naval officer and served with distinction in the Napoleonic Wars. When peace returned he took up the Admiralty challenge to find the elusive North West Passage linking the Atlantic and the Pacific. His first expedition was in 1818. Having reached Baffin Bay, he became convinced that its westward continuation was blocked by mountains and he returned home. Back in Britain he was vilified when it was later discovered that he had been deceived by a mirage. Ross was virulent in his response to criticism and spent much of his career at loggerheads with associates, including his own nephew James Clark Ross, whom he had taken on the fruitless journey.

Ross fell out of favour at the Admiralty. But, believing that he still had much to offer, he embarked on an unofficial second expedition in 1829 'as the means of effectively silencing the tongue of slander'. This one was financed largely by the gin magnate Felix Booth. Ross and his men got stuck in ice and did not manage to return home for another four years. Again he had failed to navigate the North West Passage (this was not achieved until 1906 when the Norwegian Roald Amundsen was finally successful), but valuable surveys were undertaken and James Clark Ross, the nephew with whom he had quarrelled and from whom he would again become estranged, discovered the magnetic north pole.

In the late 1840s the Admiralty spurned his proposal for an expedition to find the missing explorer Sir John Franklin. So he raised finance for the fitting out of a small vessel, which he called the *Felix* (after Felix Booth), and sailed from Stranraer on May 23, 1850. He found only graves and personal belongings.

In the 1820s Ross built as his home the North West Castle (a mock one of course) in Stranraer, now a hotel. Nautical features were incorporated into its design. He also had a home in London and it was there that he died. He was buried in Kensal Green cemetery in north-west London. His older brother Andrew Ross (1773-1812) was also a distinguished naval officer.

John Ramsay McCulloch

John Ramsay McCulloch (1789-1864) was a largely self-educated Whithorn man who became one of the leading economists of his generation with huge influence on public policy. In 1807 he went to Edinburgh University but left without a degree and took a job as a lawyer's clerk. He began reading voraciously and by 1815 he had written his first economic study, *Essay on the Question of Reducing the Interest of the National Debt*. He boldly sent it to the then pre-eminent economist David Ricardo, who approved. Thereby began a long and close association between the two men through correspondence; they only finally met face-to-face in 1823, shortly before Ricardo's death.

McCulloch joined the staff of the *Scotsman* newspaper, for which he wrote extensively on economic matters, serving as its editor between 1817 and 1821. In 1828 he became professor of political economy at the University of London. He, his Whithorn wife and their *twelve* children took up residence in fashionable Fitzroy Square. With an expensive lifestyle to maintain, McCulloch was forever on the look-out for a better-paid post, and that came in 1838 when he was appointed Comptroller of the Stationery Office, a role in which he attracted the admiration of government ministers for his success in cutting costs.

All the while he was writing books and articles, giving lectures and advising the politicians of the day. His publications were widely translated and sales added considerably to his income. In 1846 the government awarded him a state pension in recognition of his services to political economy. He was still in charge of the Stationery Office when he died of the bronchitis from which he had suffered for most of his life. He was buried in the Brompton cemetery in London, as was his wife three years later. They had been married for more than half a century.

A Wigtownshire medical practitioner making his name as a leader of Chartism, the nineteenth-century campaign for working-class enfranchisement, seems, on the face of it, an unlikely scenario. But during the 1830s and '40s that is exactly what happened to **Peter McDouall** (1814-54). He paid a heavy price: his fanatical attachment to the cause effectively ruined his career.

Peter McDouall

McDouall was born and brought up in Newton Stewart, where his father Andrew had a certain renown as 'Will Wander, the poet of the Cree' (*Will Wander of Benarrow's Trip to America and Other Poems* was published in 1832). He had a five-year apprenticeship with a local surgeon and completed his medical education in Glasgow and Edinburgh. Instead of returning home he chose to practise among the mill workers of Lancashire, settling in Ramsbottom near Bury, a one-time village that had been transformed by the Industrial Revolution.

McDouall was horrified by the working conditions of the new factory system and by their effects on the people's health. 'White slavery' he called it. It was this experience that radicalised him. Having, in the words of a contemporary, 'an ardent fiery temperament', he rose rapidly to prominence in the Chartist movement. Overcoming an initial hesitancy and nervousness, he developed into a charismatic orator, and his popularity led in 1841 to his topping the poll for election to the national committee. A fellow Chartist wrote that 'in personal appearance he was decidedly handsome' and that his centre-parted hair 'hung in long graceful curls behind his ears'. Another said that he was 'a picturesque figure... whose long cloak and general style helped to give him the appearance of a hero of melodrama'.

However, the movement was regarded by the authorities as insurrectionary and its leaders were treated as criminals. McDouall served two prison sentences, and for two years he went into protective exile in France. His obsessive political activism destroyed his professional life and, as a result, his wife Mary-Ann and their family suffered great hardship, as he himself acknowledged: 'I have been unjust to myself, negligent to my children, and forgetful of my private duties, that I might concentrate all upon the people.'

After his second period in jail he did try to resurrect his medical practice, vowing to 'retire from the talking arena'. But a colleague wisely observed that 'agitation had unfitted him for a regular life' and he was soon back on the campaign trail. His career as what he called 'a wandering, houseless lecturer' finally came to an end when he decided to emigrate to Australia in 1853. But he died shortly after arriving there. The family returned home and lived as paupers until funds gathered by Chartist sympathisers enabled Mary-Ann to set up as a stationer in Nottingham.

Sir James Caird (1816-1892) was an internationally renowned writer on agriculture whose visionary pronouncements were soundly based on his own practical experience of farming in his native Wigtownshire. Born and brought up in Stranraer, Caird briefly attended Edinburgh University before taking off for Northumberland to learn the basics of farming. Returning to Wigtownshire, he became the manager of an uncle's farm, later leasing his own on the Earl of Galloway's estate at Baldoon.

He first came to national prominence in 1849 when he entered the debate about the repeal of the Corn Laws and the consequences that free trade might bring about. In his pamphlet, *High Farming under Liberal Covenants, the Best Substitute for Protection*, he urged farmers to grow more green crops for feeding to dairy cows and for fattening beef cattle, as milk and meat were less vulnerable to overseas competition and were needed in the expanding cities.

The pamphlet brought him to central government's attention and he was invited to apply his wisdom to agriculture in post-famine Ireland. Then the *Times* newspaper commissioned him to take a hard look at English agriculture. In his findings he criticised the landowners for failing their tenants through lack of improvements and through leases that were too short.

Caird turned his attention to the USA and Canada. His views on Canada provoked, in 1859, a retaliatory pamphlet entitled *Caird's Slanders on Canada Answered and Refuted*. Other subjects on which he was asked to report included alternatives to American cotton after the Civil War broke out in 1861, and the causes of the Indian famine of 1876-7.

Meanwhile Caird had embarked on a parliamentary career. In 1852 he failed by one vote to be elected for Wigtown Burghs but at the following general election he became MP for Dartmouth in the far south-west of England. He subsequently gave up this seat in favour of Stirling Burghs, for which he was elected unopposed. All the while he was keeping his hand in at farming, only finally giving up his Baldoon tenancy in 1860 when he purchased the Cassencarie estate at Creetown in neighbouring Kirkcudbrightshire. From his new home he had the satisfaction of being able look across Wigtown Bay to the county of his birth.

Admiral Sir John Dalrymple Hay (1821-1912), naval officer and Member of Parliament, was responsible for a very loose connection between Glenluce and Napoleon Bonaparte. In his early career Hay was part of the anti-slavery patrol off the west coast of Africa. In 1834, while a young trainee, he was aboard a naval vessel that called at St Helena, where Napoleon had been exiled until his death there in 1821. Hay brought back a souvenir from the deposed emperor's grave and had it planted beside the Water of Luce. He tells the story briefly in his book of memoirs, *Lines from my Log-Books* (1898):

> The island still contained the body of the great Napoleon. I made the usual pilgrimage to the tomb, and I also brought away some cuttings from the willow, which I bought on the spot from the old French sergeant in charge, and one of them still exists as a large tree near the Bridge of Park in Wigto[w]nshire.

Dalrymple Hay's family home was at Dunragit. In 1875, for financial reasons, he had to dispose of the estate. Later he was able to build for himself a new home in the county, Craigenveoch Castle, close to Whitefield Loch south-east of Glenluce. An image of this grand house adorns the title-page of his autobiography.

Sir John McFadyean (1853-1941), the son of a Wigtownshire tenant farmer, is regarded as the founder of modern veterinary science. When he left school he worked on the family farm at Barrachan till a downturn in trade made him seek another career. He decided to build on his knowledge of farm animals by training as a vet. His bent was academic: he became a lecturer and later a professor at the Royal (Dick) School of Veterinary Studies in Edinburgh, then Principal of the Royal Veterinary College in London. Having become acutely aware of the lack of reliable information on animal anatomy, he set about filling the knowledge-gap by conducting his own detailed investigations of carcasses.

McFadyean's greatest contribution was his work on bovine tuberculosis. The outstanding expert at the time was the German bacteriologist Dr Robert Koch, who did not believe that the disease was transferable from animals to humans. McFadyean's work had shown that there was indeed a link, and in 1901 he astonished an audience in London by publicly challenging Koch on his theories. McFadyean also did valuable work on anthrax. During his career he was showered with honours, including, in 1905, his knighthood.

The Writers

At the start of the nineteenth century a Wigtownshire farmer's son **Robert Couper** (1750-1818) wrote a novel with a title that must rank as one of the oddest in the English language, *The Tourifications of Malachi Meldrum Esq* (1803). The text is just as strange.

Couper was born and raised at Balsier farm to the south of Sorbie village. He was destined for a career in the ministry, but financial hardship following the death of both his parents brought an end to his studies and he took up a tutorial post in Virginia. Returning to Scotland on the outbreak of the American War of Independence, he re-entered Glasgow University as a medical student. His first practice was in Newton Stewart. In 1788 he moved to Fochabers in Morayshire to become personal physician to the Duke of Gordon.

The Tourifications of Malachi Meldrum Esq. is a comic novel in the loose, rambling 'picaresque' style of Laurence Sterne's *Tristram Shandy* and Tobias Smollett's *The Adventures of Roderick Random*, both of which Couper must have read as a young man. He would have identified especially with Smollett, the two men having both nationality and profession in common.

The hero Malachi (more of an anti-hero) dreams of travelling to exotic places and hopes to organise his affairs so that he can take leave of absence from his farm and enjoy great adventures:

> ...my reveries were not always in unison with what was going on at the fireside. My wife, a good honest gentlewoman, and a staunch Presbyterian, was not a little disconcerted, sometimes, on hearing me, over my tankard, after supper, making little soliloquies; but when I was asking his Holiness learned questions about Rome, and the Western Church, and begging the Sublime Porte [the 10 Downing Street of the Ottoman Empire] for an account of his Revenues, and a peep into the Seraglio, the good woman I saw silently apostrophizing, and piously recommending me to the Power she thought had forgotten me.

Eventually he settles for just exploring the neighbouring counties, but he gets not much further than the nearby Saracen's Head before suffering an outbreak of gout and (after more than 400 pages!) returning home to Meldrum Hall...

> ...lamenting and grieving bitterly all the while, that my Tourifications, from which I had promised myself so much

> renown, as well as entertainment, should have terminated in less than a day, and in not more than a dozen of miles from my fire-side.

To make matters worse, during this briefest of absences the dog has died of distemper, and the author signs off with a poetic tribute 'To Poor Paulo':

> Caul, caul aneath the drappin buss,
> O Paulo! still though lies;
> Deep scrap't the bairns thy wee bit grave,
> An' wet it wi' their eyes.

The book is highly eccentric, with chapter headings like 'I ENTER UPON DUTY AS A TOURIFICATOR, AND SCIENTIFICALLY PERAMBULATE THE VILLAGE'. As for the unusual term 'tourification', it seems that Couper coined it. He is quoted by the *Oxford English Dictionary* as the first source for the word.

The work is dedicated to the Marquis of Huntly, son and heir of Couper's employer the Duke of Gordon. The following year Couper's two-volume *Poetry Chiefly in the Scottish Language* was published, and that is dedicated to Jane, Duchess of Gordon, with whom Couper had a Wigtownshire connection, she being a daughter of Sir William Maxwell of Monreith, developer of Port William.

Jane Maxwell (1748/9-1812) was one of the most remarkable women of her generation. She was renowned in the Highlands, Edinburgh and London as an ostentatious socialite. In London, where she had a home in Pall Mall, she hosted parties for the Tory circles around William Pitt and Henry Dundas. She was reputed to be one of Dundas's drinking partners, and the two of them, according to contemporary rumours, may also have been lovers. In Edinburgh she entertained Robert Burns; while, at her Highland retreat of Kinrara near Aviemore, she held seasonal gatherings that became legendary:

> Half the London world of fashion, all the clever people that could be hunted out from all parts, all the north country, all the neighbourhoods from far and near, without regard to wealth or station, and all the kith and kin of both Gordons and Maxwells, flocked to this encampment in the wilderness during the fine autumns to enjoy the free life, the pure air, and the wit and fun the duchess brought with her to the mountains.
>
> [Elizabeth Grant, *Memoirs of a Highland Lady*]

Couper, with his literary leanings and his droll sense of humour, would have fitted well into these social events. He and the duchess must also have felt comfortable together through sharing the speech of Wigtownshire. His preface to *Poetry Chiefly in the Scottish Language* contains a spirited denunciation of fashionable anglicisation in the language of Scotland. Jane, for her part, was described by a contemporary as having 'singular coarseness of speech', which in eighteenth-century 'polite' society simply meant that she continued to speak with her native accent. When she was about to marry the duke, her father told her that, once she became a duchess, she must not look down upon those who had been her equals!

After an estrangement from her husband during the 1790s Jane went into a decline. Couper left Fochabers in 1806. There were no further publications by him, and the remaining twelve years of his life are a mystery. It has to be assumed that he spent at least some of that time back home in Wigtownshire, for it was there that he died in 1818. Perhaps, after the excitement of partying with the Duchess of Gordon's set, he too had gone into a decline.

Kirkinner-born **Samuel Robinson** (1786-1874), though not a professional writer, nonetheless produced a couple of books which, thanks to recent reprints, are still read today. At the age of fourteen he sailed from Garlieston to Liverpool to join his uncle's ship that operated in the transatlantic slave trade and he recounts his adventures in *A Sailor Boy's Experiences Aboard a Slave Ship* (1867; re-issued 1996).

The book is a curious concoction. It purports to be a collection of the letters sent to family and friends in Wigtownshire from the two voyages he undertook between 1800 and 1804. But it is obvious from the pious and pompous style that, even though letters and journals of the time may have provided the basis, this raw material had been artfully re-worked in old age (he was in his 80s when the book was published).

While acknowledging the dubious morality of the slave trade, he also argues the 'well, it wasn't all that bad' case and claims that the human consignment they picked up from the west coast of Africa was relatively well treated:

> ...in fact, there is much more attention paid to the negroes during the passage, than to the crew. They get two substantial meals of fresh provision each day; if any one is taken ill, he is separated from the others, attended to by the doctor, a goat killed, and fresh soup and other good

> things given him; while the sailor never tastes anything fresh from one continent to the other, and should he be found snatching a handful of the slaves' mess when dealing it out, he would be severely punished. The picture, however, has two sides. In a few weeks the sailor can change his master, and, at least, have a chance of bettering his condition; while the poor slave is captive for life, perhaps at the mercy of a tyrant, with no relief in prospect but the grave.

Robinson vividly describes the measures taken to avoid insanitary conditions among the captives down below:

> The lower-deck, where they sleep, is kept scrupulously clean, washed and scrubbed with sand twice a week, dried with fire-pans, and fumigated with vinegar and tobacco smoke; while large tubs, with close covers, are placed at proper distances for necessary purposes. Clothes they have none – in this climate they are not required for heat, and had they any, they would very soon have more company than would be desirable.

The young Robinson is almost relieved that after two gruelling voyages he has to leave the job owing to an injury. Almost as soon as he embarked from Garlieston he was seasick: 'if ever a poor sinner was turned inside out I was that person.' By the end his juvenile romanticism about the sailor's life has been squashed:

> ...the short experience I have had of a sailor's life, has very considerably modified the opinion I had formed of it. The ocean paradise which loomed so brightly in my imagination, now appears considerably shorn of its beams. The brutal tyranny exercised by the officers, the deficiency and beggarly quality of the food and water, the isolation from everything like moral or religious training or good example, all tend to lower the fabled happiness of a sailor's life...

The book's favourable reception encouraged the elderly author to put pen to paper again, this time with an account of his Machars upbringing. This was unfortunate: *Reminiscences of Wigtonshire* (1872; re-issued 1995) is a lightweight collection of geriatric ramblings padded out with rather too many examples of his doggerel verses. Best avoided.

Sir Herbert Maxwell (1845-1937) was the most prolific Galloway author of his era, turning his fluent pen to novels, biography, to-

pography, archaeology, horticulture and both local and national history. His titles include *A History of Dumfries and Galloway* (1896), *Robert the Bruce and the Struggle for Scottish Independence* (1897), *A Life of Wellington* (1899), *A History of the House of Douglas* (1902) and *The Place Names of Galloway* (1930); while his continuous jottings on nature and antiquity were collected into seven series of *Memories of the Months* (1897-1922).

After what he called three years of 'insensate indolence' at Eton and having failed at Oxford, he returned to Wigtownshire to help run the family estate at Monreith. In 1880 he became the MP for Wigtownshire but, apparently for financial reasons, he gave up his parliamentary career in 1906 and concentrated thenceforth on his writing. His grandson Gavin Maxwell, who inherited the literary gene (see below), summed up his life thus:

> ...after an interminable and distinguished, though perhaps over-deployed, public career as politician (sometime Secretary of State for Scotland and a Lord of the Treasury), painter, archaeologist, historian, naturalist and writer of stupendous output, he departed this life as a Knight of the Thistle, Privy Councillor, Fellow of the Royal Society, Lord-Lieutenant of the County of Wigtownshire and Grand Old Man of Galloway; the possessor of a shrunken estate of 9,000 acres – and the noteworthy failure to have anything of any real value left in the house.

C H Dick, author of *Highways and Byways in Galloway and Carrick*, noted how appropriate it was that the venerable antiquarian lived where he did: 'It is a happy circumstance that the Monreith estate itself should be rich in antiquities, and that, when the proprietor discourses of standing stones, crannogs, or cup-and-ring markings, he should be able to show examples of all of these within a few minutes' walk of his house.'

Gavin Maxwell was able to observe his grandfather's way of life from the inside:

> There at Monreith, in a timeless feeling of money not actively spent but just disregarded, liveried footmen, and the fusty Victorian aura of dark wall paint and damp-stained

> bedroom ceilings, my grandfather passed his old age between his gardens and the study he had built for himself at the end of a long corridor. At the far side of this incredibly untidy room, where books were stacked everywhere on the sofas and chairs, he would sit at a big desk between two atrocious stained-glass windows, interminably writing volume after volume, answering personally all his world-wide correspondence, and contributing papers to the journals of the learned societies. The rest of the big room contained a scholar's library, glass cases full of archaeological findings, and an easel bearing whatever flower painting he was engaged upon at the moment, for he had long forsaken more general subjects to record the fabulous contents of his garden.

Here is a flavour of Sir Herbert's own writing from his introduction to *The Place-Names of Galloway*. In typical style he introduces a personal aspect, in this case the lesson that he learned about the perils of unscholarly guesswork:

> I was a very young fellow when I received a warning in that respect. On the shoulder of Barhullion Fell there is a small tarn bearing the name of Lochanour. Land drainage in comparatively recent times has so deplenished it that it disappears after a dry summer and is partly restored by autumnal rains. Its name is not entered on the Ordnance Survey map, and I first heard it spoken by a gamekeeper with whom I was out shooting. He explained that it meant 'loch in an hour, for', said he, 'an hour's rain will fill it'. I accepted this as accounting for the name, nor had I any occasion to question it until I began to give some attention to such matter. Then it became clear that the name was many centuries older than the present depleted condition of this lakelet; that it really was *lochan odhar*, the grey tarn, so named from a mass of grey glaciated rock forming its northern shore.

In the same book there is an amusing note headed 'To the Reader' in which Maxwell confesses to the shame he feels whenever he opens a work which he had written on the same subject some forty years earlier: 'that essay is so full of blunders as to render mere editing out of the question; but whereas much attention has been given in late years to the study of place-names on sound lines, I have written the whole of it afresh'. The author applied himself assiduously to the investigation of Galloway's Celtic linguistic heritage but perhaps he tried too hard, for it is interesting to see that in the more recently published *Place-Names in the*

Rhinns of Galloway and Luce Valley Professor John MacQueen writes that 'Sir Herbert Maxwell was sometimes over-enthusiastic in his pursuit of Gaelic etymologies'!

Once upon a time almost every community, it seems, had its local bard, usually a creator of insipid doggerel. Whithorn's very own McGonagall was unusual in being female. **Jeanie Donnan** (1866-1942) gets the rare honour of a memorial plaque attached to 76 George Street where she lived. This describes her as 'The Galloway Poetess'. In the early twentieth century her homespun versifying, in both Scots and English, was a regular feature in the *Galloway Gazette*. Her published collections include *Hameland* (1907), *Heatherbloom* (1911) and *The Hills o' Hame* (1930). She was evidently very popular: her first book had 500 pre-publication subscribers, headed by the Earl of Galloway. Eminent local worthies - Sir Herbert Maxwell, Sheriff Watson, Lord Sands and the Whithorn parish minister - contributed glowing forewords.

Jeanie was brought up on the Cally estate at Gatehouse of Fleet in Kirkcudbrightshire, where her father worked in the sawmill until an accident incapacitated him. Her ambition to be a teacher was thwarted by ill-health. She married young and came to live in Whithorn where her husband was a postman.

Her stuff resembles poetry in that it rhymes and scans but it is almost entirely lacking in literary merit. Her staple is the pious or sentimental platitude. One of her admirers wrote:

> ...the atmosphere of the poems is that of a world to which I fear the greater part of our population are now strangers. The voice seems to come from an older world where life was simple and more restful; where domestic joys and kindly neighbourhood seemed to fill a larger portion of it; and where youths and maidens found interest and instruction in the observation of the wonderful works of God in Nature, rather than of the wonderful works of man in films from Hollywood.

Here is the kind of verse he was thinking of:

THE NEW AGE

The kirk bell's summons rings out on the air,
But its tones I can hardly hear
For 'busses and motors that roar and clang,
To gaither thegither a motley thrang –
But no' for the kirk, I fear.

Unheeded the Sabbath's sanctity;
There are pic-nics and sporting games,
And the Auld Kirk bell noo sadly rings,
And God's left oot o' the scheme o' things,
And forgot in oor Scottish hames.

I canna believe that sich [sic] things can be
In this corner o' Galloway.
Where fair St. Medan yince sightless trod,
For her honour's sake and her troth to God,
In the ages dim and grey.

I'm maybe grown auld and got left behind,
And stand still while the age moves on.
But if that be sae I can aye hold fast
To the memories sweet o' the Sabbaths past,
And the peace o' a day that's gone.

In a piece written 'to a mother who lost three children within a few days', Jeanie offers neither insight nor empathy but cold dogma:

God comfort you, bereaved one, in your loss and anguish sore,
You dearly loved your little ones, but Jesus loved them more,
So tenderly He loved them, He claimed them for His own,
To swell the choir of Angels who sing around the throne.

The drivel continues:

Oh cease your bitter sobbing, and still your restless fears,
You are hidden from your darlings by a mist of blinding tears;
Up yonder they are waiting in their robes of spotless white,
To tell you of their happy home among the Angels bright.

Gavin Maxwell (1914-1969), still best remembered for accounts of his life with otters, *Ring of Bright Water* (1960) and *The Rocks Remain* (1963), developed his fascination for the natural world as he tramped the moors around his Wigtownshire childhood home within his grandfather's Monreith estate. He wrote about his upbringing in *The House of Elrig* (1965). Like most of the offspring of the Scottish landed gentry, Maxwell was sent away to be educated within the English private system, but throughout his term-time absences he pined for his Machars paradise. He grew to adore Hannam, the family's gamekeeper, despite being squeamish about the killing of creatures:

> …the sight of one of his great boat-shaped boots crushing a curled-up hedgehog newly released from a gin-trap; of a stoat that in its efforts to break free had almost chewed through one of its forelegs, only to be killed now by a blow from Hannam's stick; of a magpie not quite dead from strychnine poisoning sucked from a doctored hen's egg; all these things produced in me a revulsion that for the time being survived Hannam's rationalisations. 'They all come to die,' he would say, 'there's no mercy in nature, and like as not their natural deaths'd be worse'n that. The stoat eats the rabbit alive, screaming away for twenty minutes or more, and he'll kill maybe a thousand rabbits in his lifetime. And if a hawk can gets its feet on a young stoat he's not bothering whether his claws go in the guts or the heart or whether the beast's dead when he starts eating. Na, na. A man doesn't like to see suffering, but it's there whether he looks at it or not.'

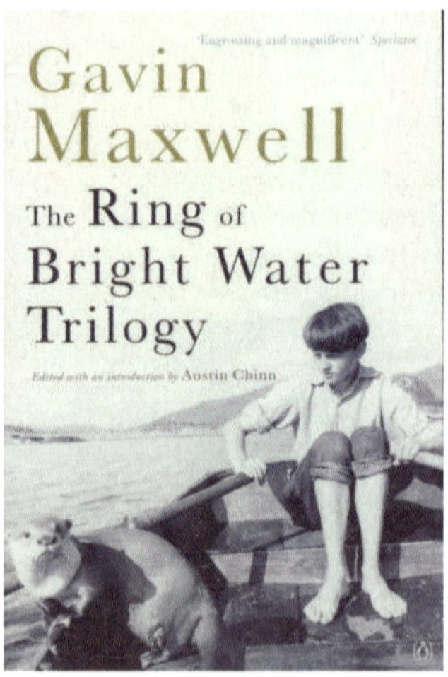

There was much excitement in 1969 when the author appeared at the cinema in Newton Stewart to introduce a showing of the film based on *Ring of Bright Water*. In the *Galloway Gazette* a report on his visit was surrounded by advertisements exploiting the otter theme. A local baker, for example, boasted 'Our Cream Cakes "Otter" Be Good'!

Less well known than his love-affair with otters was Maxwell's infatuation with wild geese, wintering visitors to his grandfather's estate. He wrote about them in his last book *Raven Seek Thy Brother* (1968):

> Their origins went far back in my life, to the days before the war, when I had built up at Monreith a collection of the wild geese of the world; when Snow Geese from North America and Bar-headed Geese from Tibet grazed the grassy slope below the old castle and the garden itself held exotic rarities. There had been the little Lesser Whitefronts that I had myself brought back from Lapland the last summer before the war; they would answer to their names with a shrill clamour…There had been a Cape Barren Goose, I remember, who would walk in through the open french windows of the library and squat in front of the fire, her delicate dove-grey, argus-eyed plumage quivering with contentment, and

> at the hour of the evening flight the air would be full of the wild wings and the desolate music of the Greylags and the Snow Geese from the loch.

There is a Gavin Maxwell memorial, unsurprisingly in the shape of an otter, on the cliffs close to Monreith Bay. Part of the inscription is in Latin: *'Haec Loca Puer Amavit – Vir Celebravit'*. A translation is provided: 'This place he loved as a boy – and made famous as a man'. An inspection in 2007 revealed that some wag had removed the 'as' from the first part of the translation to make a joke about Maxwell's sexual interest in his own gender: 'This place he loved a boy...'!

Wigtown Ploughman (1939) by **John McNeillie** (1916-2002) is a local novel that caused a sensation when it was published and then serialised in a Sunday tabloid as 'The Story that has Startled Scotland'. The newspaper commented that 'Seldom, if ever, has the rural population of Scotland evinced such interest in a novel'. The book presents a brazenly unsentimental view of farming life in the Machars, shocking in its descriptions of degeneracy and drunken debauchery. It was a fiery young man's literary debut and the furore around its publication brought instant fame to McNeillie at the age of just twenty-two.

The story centres on the brutish upbringing of Andy Walker. His father, also Andy, is a wife-batterer, while his mother Sarah is a slut. The couple have already had several children out of wedlock when they finally get married. This is a flavour of the wedding celebration:

> Some were sick, all, even the pale-faced children, were drunk. There was laughter and ribaldry until the early hours of the morning, and Andy was not sure for a week or two whether his wife had slept her first night with him or one of his bosom cronies.

While the father is out working in the fields, the mother manages to combine looking after the children with entertaining her lovers:

> Sarah, an unintelligent creature herself, thought it a waste of time to send them to school, but they were out of the way when things not for their eyes to see, or for their tongues to betray, took place in her husband's absence. There were herds [shepherds] who sometimes called when passing the lonely cothouse; a burly grocer gave her provisions, and asked for no money!

Eventually Sarah ceases to care about what the children may see:

> When Andy was very young, Sarah allowed him to remain in bed with her and her latest lover. He lay and cried at the foot of the bed, and was usually silenced with a kick or two. Once he had been badly burnt when playing on the floor; he slipped and his hands grasped the bars of the grate. Sarah had been too slow to disentangle herself from a fond embrace, and the marks remained on his hands all his life.

McNeillie knew that the book would cause ripples but he defiantly ended his foreword with a simple, provocative question: 'Would you have me tell you a fairy story?' In the copy that he sent to his blacksmith grandfather in Wigtownshire he wrote: 'May you read it, enjoy & understand it, and if at times, like Robbie Burns, I have taken liberties and shocked the modesty of those who open its pages to read it, I hope they will forgive me.' Some folk never did forgive him. According to his son Andrew, who has published a moving memoir of his father, *Wigtown Ploughman* was both loved and loathed in the Shire: 'One side couldn't put the book down, while the other couldn't wait to do so'. McNeillie's publisher exploited the furore with an advertising campaign for 'A Violent Novel that has roused the Lowlands'.

John McNeillie was not a Wigtownshire man by birth. He came originally from Dalmuir near Glasgow. After a sister died in an outbreak of meningitis, he was sent at a very young age to live in the fresh air of the south-west with his paternal grandparents at North Clutag Farm, west of Bladnoch. The chance to observe nature at close-hand had a profound effect on his character and outlook, and his childhood memories formed the bedrock theme for the rest of his long literary career.

Given the intensity of his obsession with the Shire, it is remarkable that in fact he spent barely five years with his grandparents. He re-joined his parents for a family move to Southall in west London. For a ten-year-old boy the contrast between the Machars and Middlesex could not have been more dramatic. At school he was tauntingly referred to as 'the haggis' and, in the words of his biographer son, he 'learnt fast to call a mavis a thrush, a laverock a skylark, and glaur mud, and proved a wise chameleon'.

McNeillie went on to write another forty or so books, as well as a prodigious amount of journalism, mainly on country matters and most notably for *Country Life* to which he regularly contributed 'A Countryman's Notes' for some forty years. The most enduring has been *The Poacher's Handbook* ('for the man with the hare-pocket and the boy with the snare'), first published in 1950 and since then never out-of-print.

Almost all of this later output was under the pen-name of 'Ian Niall'. It is often assumed that this pseudonym was designed as an escape from his scandalous association with *Wigtown Ploughman*. In fact its origin was rather more practical. His original publisher wanted him to re-write parts of his novel about travelling folk, *No Resting Place*. McNeillie refused and, using the Ian Niall name, sent the manuscript to a rival publisher, who duly issued it in 1948 as the work of a newly discovered author, though by then McNeillie already had three published novels to his credit. From then until his death at the age of eighty-five he remained, in literary terms, Ian Niall.

After the boyhood move to Middlesex, McNeillie spent the rest of his long life away from Scotland. There was a long period in north Wales, at Old Colwyn and later Llandudno, followed by retirement to a house inherited by his wife in the Chilterns of southern England. Of this final resting-place his obituarist in the *Independent* wrote that 'he regarded the environment as suburban and, while he gloomily shot the grey squirrels which were damaging his trees, he hankered for the high hills of Wales'.

His deepest hankering, though, was always for that brief but intense childhood idyll at North Clutag. Any notion that the sourness of *Wigtown Ploughman* reflected his years there is thoroughly dispelled by the affectionate tone of his autobiographical *A Galloway Childhood* (1967). The warmth of his recollection rises from every page. He concludes: 'I need not say that as a child in Galloway I was happy and that although I have been happy since I have never been happier than I was then.' Here's a typical passage:

> The biblical description of a land of milk and honey took my imagination from the moment I first heard it. It seemed to me that I lived in this land, and in a way I did, for I was well used to the sight of great bowls of cream skimmed from the milk to make butter, to the very smell of milk and the intestinal rumblings of ruminating cows waiting to be hur-

> ried down the road to the pasture when milking was over, and to the scent and taste of honey. Milk and honey are two of the oldest harvests of man, sweet, rich and natural. Samson fed on honey and look what he did with the jawbone of an ass!

Looking back, he confesses to a strong strain of nostalgia:

> The Galloway of my childhood is no more. The people who belonged in it have gone. No one who writes about life does life justice by being a realist. The fields were greener, the trees were taller, the spots on the trout I caught were the most brilliant red you could ever imagine, and the curlew's cry would have broken your heart and you will never hear its like, now or ever. You must take my word for that.

Though he thought about the Shire incessantly, in later life he re-visited only to see an elderly aunt in Kirkinner. He could not bear to see the changes that had taken place, as he made clear in reply to a letter from an admirer of *A Galloway Childhood*:

> The green centred road to Alticry is all tarred now and cars flash along past the lodges on the way. There are no rabbits in the roadside bracken, no black grouse cackling, no bilberries to be picked across the road from Glenling and the school up there, like Malzie school, is closed. The old men of Brachan and Mochrum are not the old men of my childhood and it is all too sad to bear. Once there would be hens on the street in Mochrum, sleeping dogs, and old women talking, while the fires burned peat and time stood still. Nobody knows what I carry in my mind!

In the same letter he makes the startling statement that 'I should have died then and life would have been perfect!'

In the end all the controversy about the county's reputation in the light of *Wigtown Ploughman* was forgotten. Today McNeillie's exposé of living conditions in rural Wigtownshire is hailed for its galvanising effect upon local politicians, and the man himself is now venerated as a local treasure. Wigtown's refurbished County Buildings house the John McNeillie Library, while the town's County Hotel has had its name changed to the Wigtown Ploughman Hotel.

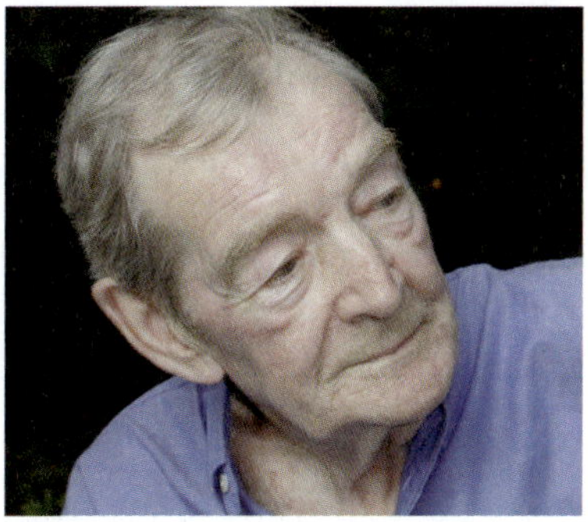

Alastair Reid, the Wigtownshire-bred poet, essayist and translator, was born in 1926 at Whithorn where his father was the kirk minister and his mother a doctor. His studies at St Andrews University were interrupted by naval service in the Second World War. When he returned 'I had seen the Mediterranean, the Red Sea, the Indian Ocean, and enough ports of call, enough human variety, to make St Andrews seem small and querulous.'

Thereafter Reid made a point of never being permanently rooted, setting up a succession of temporary homes in the USA, France, Spain, Switzerland and both Central and South America, 'resting places only, places eventually to move on from'. The principal constant in his life has been employment with *The New Yorker* magazine. In his early 70s he could still write: '*The New Yorker* remains my only address, one fixed point in my shifting existence.' In *Oases* (1997), a collection of pieces described as 'the essence of Alastair Reid', he compares his own wanderlust with the entrenchment of those he left behind:

> I have a friend in Scotland, a painter, who still lives in the fishing town he was born in, grew up in, went to school in, was married in, raised his children in, works in, and clearly intends to die in. I look on him with uncomprehending awe, for although I had much the same origins that he had, born and sprouting in rural Scotland, close to the sea, living more by the agrarian round than by outside time, I had in my head from an early age the firm notion of leaving, long before I knew why or how.

Wigtownshire remains in his mind, however, as one of the 'oases' of his life:

> ...a gentle, kindly beginning, for we were bound by the rhythms of the soil, always outdoors, helping at neighbouring farms, haunting small harbours, looking after animals, or romping in the oat and barley fields...as often as not, my parents' stipends would come in the form of oats, potatoes, eggs, and game. When my father, from the pulpit, read of 'a land flowing with milk and honey', I was overcome by the beauty of the image, and had no doubt at all that he was talking about where we lived...

The best of Reid's poems were collected in *Weathering* (1978) and again in *Inside Out* (2008). In their global range of subject-matter the Shire is not forgotten. 'Whithorn Manse' describes a rueful return visit:

> I knew it as Eden,
> that lost walled garden,
> past the green edge
> of priory and village;
> and, beyond it, the house,
> withdrawn, white,
> one window alight.
>
> Returning, I wonder,
> idly, uneasily,
> what eyes from inside
> look out now, not in,
> as once mine did,
> and what might grant me
> a right of entry?
>
> *Is it never dead, then,*
> *that need of an Eden?*
>
> Even this evening,
> estranged by age,
> I ogle that light
> with a child's greed,
> wistfully claiming
> lost prerogatives
> of homecoming.

Donald MacIntosh is another Wigtownshire man who has spent most of his adult life in exile but has remained deeply nostalgic about the way of life that formed his character. His *Travels in Galloway* (1999) is a book of memoirs about a Machars childhood in the 1930s/40s. Brought up near Garlieston, MacIntosh trained as a forester and much of his career was in the rain-forests of west Africa. He recalls the long, cold winter nights of Wigtownshire and the lack of entertainment:

> A weekly visit to the pub for a pint and a game of darts was about the optimum in social activity for most men, and

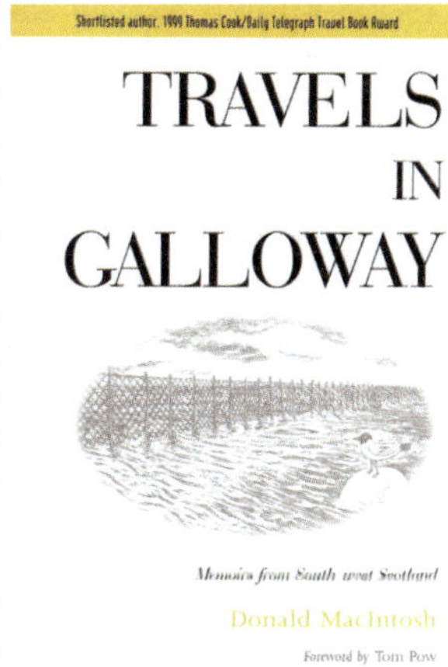

even then it often meant cycling two or three miles over exposed moorland tracks in driving sleet and rain to their adopted hostelries...while the women had what the men often unkindly referred to as 'the bliddy Rural'. The Women's Rural Institute was probably what kept a lot of country women sane, for theirs was the toughest job of all. Looking after the home in those days was a full-time occupation, and this weekly escape must have been a much-looked-forward-to event for them. Part of the attraction was undoubtedly the fact that the in-fighting at some of the 'bliddy Rurals' could be as intense and as bitter (and, therefore, as entertaining) as at any political gathering at Westminster. Committee elections were often savagely contested, and those who won competitions such as 'Best Knitted Socks' and 'Best Clootie Dumpling' could be sure that, while they might secretly bask for a long time in the glow that would result from the accolades to their triumphs in the 'WRI Activities' columns of the Galloway Gazette, somewhere out there in the sticks the inevitable javelins would be getting sharpened...

Wigtown-based author **Donna Brewster** began researching the history of her home in the town's Station Road and the outcome was *The House that Sugar Built* (1999). The house in question is now called Dunure but was known as Barbados Villa when it was built in the 1830s by John McGuffie, a former saddler from Mochrum who made a fortune in Barbadian sugar. Returning to his native county as a man of substance, McGuffie became Provost of Wigtown and was still in office when he died in 1861. But the most intriguing character in the story is McGuffie's mixed-race Barbadian daughter Margaret, who came to live with him in the house and, after her father's death, stayed on there until her own death in 1896. Barbados Villa came to be known locally as 'the dark lady's house'. The book, based on fact but written as fiction, portrays Margaret's loneliness as an exotic incomer who did not find it easy to be accepted into Wigtown society:

> Servants did not openly defy her, nor did shopkeepers completely disregard her, but her orders were not treated as priority. Her commands were obeyed a little less quickly than those of her father; her business was attended to with a casual air; curtsies were none too deep; faces were pulled behind her back; giggles were stifled less than efficiently.
>
> Her father's people were kind and welcoming to her but she remained, even after twenty years, a family curiosity. No matter how hard she tried to blend, to think and be like them, she was not. When they gathered with McGuffies, her father reverted immediately and unconsciously to the broader accents of his childhood. The family sang songs together that she did not know, and they did not take time to teach her; they quoted poetry that she could not understand, and they did not explain; they used words, quaint little Galloway expressions, that she had never heard and, when she looked puzzled, they laughed together gleefully. She knew that they did not mean to be cruel, but, every time they laughed, a deeper wedge was driven between her and the people who called themselves her family.

There are two other Wigtownshire historical novels by Donna Brewster: *Second Daughter* (1989) about the Covenanters and *My Ninian* (2006).

The Movies

For many centuries Wigtownshire has been a place of pilgrimage because of its association with the saintly Christian missionary Ninian. Nowadays pilgrims of a different kind also arrive in the county in substantial numbers every year. They want to see not where Ninian prayed but where a strange movie called *The Wicker Man* was shot.

When *The Wicker Man* – starring Diane Cilento, Britt Ekland, Christopher Lee and Edward Woodward - was released in 1973 it almost immediately bombed at the box-office. Yet somehow or another it got a second coming as a kind of cultish interest. Its story of pleasure-seeking paganism caught on among devotees of 'alternative' living. Now enthusiasts coming to the area to follow the location trail make a not inconsiderable contribution to the region's tourism trade, a phenomenon given an extra boost through the movie having inspired the creation of an annual music event called the Wickerman Festival. This takes place in neighbouring Kirkcudbrightshire, which also provided the film-makers with a range of picturesque backdrops.

The film's action is supposed to take place on an island off the north-west coast of Scotland but, when the sums had been done, mainland Galloway proved to be a more feasible option for a crew on a limited budget. The time of year is meant to be spring but the filming actually took place at the start of winter so for some scenes the bare trees had to be festooned with fake blossom.

The story centres on Sgt Howie (Edward Woodward), a seriously Christian police officer who is sent to investigate the case of a missing girl. To his horror he finds himself to be amongst a community of weirdos who eventually have him and an assortment of animals sacrificially burnt inside the 'wicker man'. This climactic scene was shot at Burrow Head, the southern tip of the Machars peninsula. The huge human-shaped pyre, made from wicker fencing panels, was constructed on location. A second, smaller version was also built for the shooting of close-ups once the main one had been incinerated. After the building work was finished, the set designer was still not satisfied with the landscaping:

> It looked too flat, it needed scale and contrast. It was a strain on the budget and on manpower but I asked the team to find a tree, an old, tortured, mysterious-looking tree, and bring it to the site no matter what. So they drove around, found the right tree, dug it up and brought it to Burrow Head, where we replanted it.

Woodward later claimed that he had not previously been told that he would be inside the wicker man when it was set alight. He described the experience as 'really frightening'. Fortunately, as the conflagration intensified, he was replaced by a stunt-man lowered in from a cherry-picker. While still inside the burning effigy the actor had some consolation: 'At least it was warm, especially when the goats above urinated on me in terror'. Woodward recalled the challenging weather conditions:

> The wind was so astonishing. I remember putting a cigarette in my mouth, lighting it and it just went all the way down...You got through an awful lot of cigarettes like that; you didn't get many puffs because you didn't get the chance to.

Other Wigtownshire settings included Logan Botanic Garden, Stranraer, Whithorn and Lochinch Castle, home of the Earl of Stair. This is what Diane Cilento remembered in particular about their time at Lochinch:

> Lord Stair invited the whole cast to a banquet one night at the castle, a very lavish do, very formal. At the end of the evening, the ladies had to retire while the men enjoyed their cigars and port. We were in this drawing-room getting a bit bored so we went out to the balcony. We looked sideways to the next balcony along – and there were all the men from the film peeing off the balcony into the gardens.

The cold weather seems to have made the actors and crew pretty miserable much of the time. No one more so than Britt Ekland. She had an extra reason of her own for being down in the dumps. Almost none of her colleagues knew at the time that she had just discovered she was pregnant by her then boyfriend. In the absence of the boyfriend she felt alone and anxious. She did not enjoy staying at the Kirroughtree Hotel near Newton Stewart, where she had to use a shared bathroom, and she was not impressed by Newton Stewart itself. In an interview with a Sunday newspaper she described the place as being full of hardened drinkers: it 'had to be the most dismal place in Creation...one of the bleakest places I've been to in my life.' The publication of her views caused a local furore. Through the *Galloway Gazette* the town's provost hit back: 'She comes from Sweden and what are they noted for? Illegitimacy, promiscuity and permissiveness.' As for drink, the provost added: 'I saw Miss Ekland at various functions. She seemed capable of downing great quantities of drink.' The film's producer was forced to issue a conciliatory statement:

> Any goosepimples which our Sassenach skins suffered during our stay with you were quickly smoothed away by the warmth of our personal relationships with you. I would like to dissociate all of us from the comments made by Miss Ekland and I hope you will accept my own personal apology.

Ekland had been cast, more for her looks than for her acting ability, as Willow MacGregor, the sexy daughter of the pub landlord. Her strong Swedish accent was a considerable obstacle. In a later dubbing session she attempted to re-do her dialogue with a Scottish accent. But the result was embarrassingly bad and, without Ekland's knowledge at the time and to her subsequent dismay, the Scottish actress and jazz singer Annie Ross was brought in during post-production to provide the final version of Willow's voice.

Not only do we not hear Ekland's voice; it is also not entirely her own body that we see in the notorious nude scene. 'She was perfectly prepared to show her tits,' the director Robin Hardy explained years later, 'but we had to get a night-club go-go dancer very quickly to play her backside.'

Several days before filming began a convoy carrying some seventy crew members trundled into Newton Stewart and recruitment of locals as extras got underway. Beside a picture of the film-trucks the *Galloway Gazette* reported:

> It was actually King Street, Newton Stewart, but it might have been Sunset Boulevard, Broadway as 'Hollywood hopefuls' beat a path to the door of Douglas House on Monday evening. That was the scene of the British Lion auditions for their film *The Wicker Man.* Many a top star got into pictures the same small way, after all. As sisters Muriel and Julia Duncan, of Boreland Farm, Whauphill, explained: 'We've always wanted to see a film star in the flesh. And now that we've got a chance of actually appearing in a picture along with them, well, we've just told Dad he'll have to manage the farm without us for the next few weeks.'

Robin Hardy, for whom this was a directorial debut, wanted to spice up the film with as much nudity as possible. But when it came to shooting the Fire Dance Girls a colleague successfully called for a sense of decency:

> I said to him, if Ken Russell and Sam Peckinpah can't get away with showing naked under-age girls in their films,

> what makes you think you can, on a film made in a conservative part of Scotland?

In the event the modesty of the young locals was maintained by issuing them with body-stockings, albeit somewhat flimsy ones!

At least two other films made for the cinema have Wigtownshire as a setting, in both cases Portpatrick.

Hunted (1952) starred Dirk Bogarde and was directed by Charles Crichton, who had had huge success the previous year with his now classic comedy *The Lavender Hill Mob*.

Chris Lloyd (Bogarde) is on the run after murdering his wife's lover. He meets up with a young Scots orphan boy Robbie (Jon Whiteley) who is so frightened of his foster parents in London that when he accidentally sets some curtains on fire he scarpers. Lloyd tries to send the boy back home but they become attached to each other and escape to Scotland together. The police naturally assume that Robbie has been kidnapped. The plan in Portpatrick is to flee aboard a stolen fishing-boat but Lloyd, who at heart is a decent man, decides to return and give himself up in the interests of Robbie's welfare.

The *Evening Standard* review said: 'The one feature of *Hunted* that saves it from the trite is the presence of a six-year-old Scottish lad named Jon Whiteley'; while the *Observer*'s view was: 'The discipline involved in playing with and to a child seems to have found new reserves of strength in Dirk Bogarde's acting.'

This was the movie debut of Whiteley, the son of an Aberdeen headmaster. His talent was discovered when he read 'The Owl and the Pussy-Cat' on radio. The bonding between him and Bogarde in the story was reflected in a warm relationship off-screen. 'He treated me as if he was an older brother,' Whiteley recalled in later life. Bogarde took him to toyshops and as a parting gift at the conclusion of the shoot he gave him a Tri-ang tractor and trailer, though the boy had actually requested a monkey from Harrods' pet shop!

Whiteley and Bogarde were re-united five years later for *The Spanish Gardener* (1956), an adaptation of the A J Cronin novel. Their earlier off-the-set rapport was never re-captured. By this time Whiteley was a slightly priggish eleven-year-old and Bogarde's growing stardom had turned him pompous and self-regarding. After the completion of this second project together they never met again. Indeed some forty years later Whiteley's fond memories were soured by a television interview that the homosexual Bogarde gave towards the end of his life. To Whiteley's astonishment Bogarde claimed his juvenile co-star had been the unwanted child of elderly parents and that he had contemplated adopting him. 'It was mind-boggling rubbish,' said Whiteley. 'I thought he must have been talking about somebody else...There was no bearing on reality at all.' Whiteley's mother said it was 'degrading to the family to suggest such a thing'.

Through the two Bogarde movies and some others Jon Whiteley enjoyed a period as a phenomenally successful child actor. At the Academy Awards of 1955 he was given an honorary juvenile Oscar for his part in *The Kidnappers* (1953). His film career came to an orderly end. His father had agreed to it on condition that he gave up at the age of eleven and got down to the serious business of being educated. Whiteley did exactly that and he ended up as a distinguished art historian based at the Ashmolean Museum in Oxford – cataloguing pictures rather than appearing in them!

Forty years after *Hunted*, movie trucks re-appeared in Portpatrick, this time for ***Double X: The Name of the Game*** (1992). Some scenes were also shot among the ruins of nearby Dunskey Castle.

A former Chicago cop, holidaying in a Scottish fishing village, meets up with an Englishman whose daughter has been kidnapped by a criminal gang. The film starred Norman Wisdom, for whom it was a return to the big screen after a long absence. It was also an unusually serious role for a man who is more readily associated with slapstick comedy.

Other Pairs of Eyes

During the past two hundred years or so a wide range of notable writers have recorded their impressions of Wigtownshire, from poets like John Keats and Edwin Muir to dedicated travellers such as George Borrow in the nineteenth century and H V Morton in the twentieth. The county has featured prominently in one of the great classics of Scottish fiction by James Barke, while also attracting the attention of the crime storytellers Freeman Wills Crofts and, more recently, Aline Templeton. And a most unexpected vision of Wigtownshire came during the 1940s from the palette of Austrian artist Oskar Kokoschka.

The walking-tour of southern Scotland undertaken in 1818 by the English poet **John Keats** brought him through Wigtownshire. While in the area he took a return trip across to northern Ireland. Writing to his brother from the other side of the North Channel, he compared the Scottish character unfavourably with that of the Irish, citing the difference of personality between the Scottish women whom he had encountered and his Irish chambermaid:

> She is fair, kind and ready to laugh, because she is out of the horrible dominion of the Scotch Kirk. A Scotch girl stands in terrible awe of the Elders – poor little Susannas – they will scarcely laugh – they are greatly to be pitied and the Kirk is greatly to be damn'd...These Kirkmen have done Scotland harm – they have banished puns and laughing and kissing...

Returning to Portpatrick and resuming the letter to his brother, Keats comments on the superiority of Wigtownshire in one respect:

> ...in Ireland we had too much opportunity to see the worse than nakedness, the rags, the dirt and misery of the poor common Irish. A Scotch cottage, though in that sometimes the smoke has no exit but at the door, is a palace to an Irish one.

Having sampled both sides of the Sheuch, Keats noted, as visitors commonly do to this day, the similarity in accent of the two peoples (see The Irish Connection).

On their way to the Rhins coast for the Irish crossing Keats and his companion had stopped overnight at Glenluce, where they dined 'on dirty bacon dirtier eggs and dirtiest Potatoes with a slice of salmon'. The following morning (July 6) was brilliantly hot and they went to take a look at the remains of Glenluce Abbey. Keats's response was tersely dismissive: 'they were scarcely worth the while.'

It was also a hot July when the literary traveller **George Borrow** passed through Glenluce during his walk across Galloway in 1866. He recorded his general impression in his journal:

> The land seemed to be very poor and sterile. Saw at last a kind of lake on my right hand, apparently about three hundred yards across. A cottage stood near it, and seeing a woman engaged in weeding a garden I entered into conversation with her. We first talked about the weather, and she told me that the crops had suffered much from drought, but that some rain had lately fallen which had done much good. I praised the country, but she did not agree with me, saying it was a 'coorse country'. She spoke in the broadest Galloway dialect, and I had the greatest difficulty in understanding what she said.

(See Glenluce, Kirkcowan and Stairhaven in Part 1 for more details of Borrow's journey).

Wigtownshire features substantially in *Sir John Magill's Last Journey* (1930), a crime novel by **Freeman Wills Crofts**. Sir John, an Ulster businessman returning home from London, takes the 'Paddy' ferry train from Euston to Stranraer but disappears during the journey. Inspector French of Scotland Yard is put onto the case along with Detective Sergeant Adam M'Clung of the Royal Ulster Constabulary. The trail of clues brings the two of them to Portpatrick:

> French, who had never been there before, was agreeably surprised. 'The next time I want a quiet holiday', he told M'Clung, 'this is the place for me.'
>
> 'It used to be a more important place than it is now', M'Clung observed. 'In old times it was the port for the north of Ireland. I remember my grandfather telling me about his seeing the mail packet sailing from here to Donaghadee. See the money that's been spent on this harbour and it's

> the same at Donaghadee. Only there the place is half silted up'

Inspector French has to visit Ulster, leaving Loch Ryan on the ferry for Larne:

> In the early sunshine of that autumn morning the surroundings of the loch struck him as quite beautiful. The shores, particularly on the starboard side, rose gently into bare rounded hills, which grew wilder and rockier as they approached the open sea. Between were wooded valleys which French no sooner saw than he longed to explore. But it was the colouring that appealed most to him, the dark greens of grass and leaves, shaded here and there to grays and russets, the golden browns of heather and bracken, the darker tints of rock, turning almost to black at the base of the cliffs, the thin blue of the sky and the steel gray of the water, all these were presented with the soft rich tones of the western atmosphere. Then out into the open sea, with the sugar loaf of Ailsa Craig standing blue and sharp on the northern horizon and the Irish coast a faint line right ahead.

Arriving in Ulster, Inspector French 'saw that the Irish side was nearly, if not quite, as beautiful as the Scotch'.

According to *In Scotland Again* (1933), the indefatigable travel writer **H V Morton** became increasingly enchanted as he journeyed from the Stewartry into the Shire:

> I would like to gather together a crowd of people who are tired of cities and take them through Galloway. There would be bright days when we would walk that lovely coast road from Gatehouse of Fleet to Newton Stewart. We would take all the by-roads, get lost, sit on stone walls and tell stories, admire the 'belties', lean over bridges and watch brown burn water flowing.
>
> At Newton Stewart we would cross the bridge over the Cree and envy the people who live in houses which go straight down to the water, as they do in Venice. It would be grand to lie in bed and fish! We would find the little inn where the pretty girl says shyly that the water isna verra guid, but the beer's fine.

Morton rated Newton Stewart as 'one of the bonniest little towns in the whole of Galloway' (see Part 1 – Newton Stewart), while at Wigtown he noted a certain melancholy emanating from its maritime decline (see Part 1 – Wigtown). Moving onto the Mull of Galloway, he felt almost as if he had crossed water:

> It is the extremity of a long slender strip about thirty miles in length that, but for the narrow neck of land between Glenluce and Stranraer, would be a little island off the coast of Wigtownshire. It has, like all out-of-the-way places, an island atmosphere. It reminds me very much of the Lleyn Peninsula in Wales.
>
> I went there on a lovely windy morning, with the salt waters breaking over the splendid Sands of Luce. I found myself in a soft, gentle land of woods and broad fields continually swept by sea winds. The Rhinns of Galloway... have a character of their own; and I imagine that ways of speech and habits, long vanished from what one thinks of as 'the mainland', are to be found here among the secluded little lanes and the lonely white farms.

In *Scottish Journey* (1935) the Orkney- and Glasgow-bred poet **Edwin Muir** motors across the Moors of northern Wigtownshire and is spellbound:

> It is difficult to give any impression of that beautiful and almost quite solitary stretch of moorland that lies between Newton Stewart and the bleak village of Barrhill in the south of Ayrshire. For about twenty miles I can remember seeing only two houses. On every side the moorland flowed away in low waves to the horizon, except where it was broken, far away in the east, by the dark mountains of Galloway. There was no sign of life, except for a few distant sheep nibbling the harsh tufts of grass that grew here and there among the heather; even birds did not seem to come here, and the only sound I heard was of one lark singing far up. The thin air was sweetened by a thousand scents rising into it from every tuft in these miles of moorland, mingling as they rose, so that one seemed to be breathing in the landscape itself, drinking it in with all one's senses except that of hearing, which was magically stilled. The silence of such places is so complete that it sinks into one's mind in waves, making it clearer and clearer, drenching it as with a potion concocted out of some positive life-giving essence, not out of the mere absence of sound.

Wigtownshire is the most significant of the settings for *Land of the Leal* (1939), **James Barke**'s huge and passionate family saga of late-nineteenth/early-twentieth-century Scotland. Though reared largely in Fife, Barke knew Wigtownshire through family connections and almost half of the novel's 600-plus pages are devoted to the county.

Based on the experiences of his parents, both of whom had been farm workers in dairying, the book portrays the decline in traditional country life and the spread of industrialisation. The picture it paints of the Rhins is stridently unromantic. For most of the farm workers, exploited by greedy landowners, life is harsh and virtually cheerless. The only escapes from the drudgery are religion and alcohol. The worst lot is that of the women, who die prematurely, worn out by continuous child-bearing. Barke was a Socialist and his identification with the oppressed is fervent:

> The farmers dominated the life of the countryside and the farmers in their turn were dominated by the landlords. The people had no life. Their best hours were given to the labour of the land. When their work was over they retired to their cot-houses – miserable one-roomed boxes, many of them built of turf-sods without windows of any kind – and there partook of their porridge or gruel and crawled into bed or threw themselves down on a bunch of straw or hay in a corner.

The central character David Ramsay vows to leave in search of a better life for his wife and family. He is sick of kowtowing to the employers:

> And what did the farmers do with their money? Kept it in the bank to grow even more. Money! there was no lack of it in Kirkmaiden – dairy-farming was paying. The new creamery at Dunragit was paying. Milk was money. The land was flowing with milk and money. And yet poverty stalked everywhere. The agricultural labourers were almost on the level of starvation...He would need to get out of the Rhinns, need to make an escape somehow before he was finally and fully enslaved.

His new life in Glasgow is not much better, but a holiday back in Wigtownshire convinces him that a return to his roots would be no good either:

> ...he dreaded going back to Glasgow, dreaded more than anything going back into the shipyard with its noise and clamour and dirt. Nor did it help to reassure him to realise

> that there was nothing for him or his family in his native Galloway. He felt it would be an agony to come back and work in a land whose physical features had remained unaltered but whose spirit had withered and decayed.

Detective Inspector Marjory Fleming, a Wigtownshire police officer and farmer's wife, is the central character in a series of crime novels by **Aline Templeton**: *Cold in the Earth* (2005), *The Darkness and the Deep* (2006), *Lying Dead* (2007) and *Lamb to the Slaughter* (2008). The locations are composites of real places in the county: 'Kirkluce' is between Stranraer and Newton Stewart; 'Knockhaven' is on the Machars coast near Port William; and 'Drumbreck' lies on the Cree estuary close to Wigtown.

The first book in the series centres on the foot-and-mouth crisis of 2001. In an interview the author explained why:

> It happened by chance. I knew the plot for my new book, which involved bulls, and I knew what my detective was like, in personality. I went down to Wigtown to do an event when the foot-and-mouth epidemic was at its height and I was very much struck by the horror of it all – nothing living in the fields, no sheep on the hills, a sort of dead landscape. I began to think how awful it would be for the police force in such a close-knit community, having to force people they knew well to allow the killing-squads on to their land to wipe out stock lines which had perhaps been bred for generations, and then what a terrible dilemma it would be if you were actually married to a farmer.

In the story DI Fleming starts to feel the pressure:

> She'd worked a twelve-hour shift – not particularly unusual, except that this one had imposed an emotional strain which had left her feeling so drained and exhausted that she barely felt able to get out of the car.
>
> Six hours of it had been spent at Bob Christie's farm, shouting at first through a loudhailer, an operation that had left her throat raw. Eventually, she had persuaded him on to the phone, then at last got him outside to talk. He was defiant at first, defeated at last after hours of patient discussion. They had confiscated his shotguns, escorted the slaughter team in to do their work, and she had seen the bluff, cheery farmer she had known...reduced to a sobbing, shivering wreck by the agents of the state, of which she was one.

As the livestock are eliminated from the farms, she sees a

change in the landscape:

> ...there in the pastures, when you looked closer, were rank grasses, nettles, docks and sorrel, the ungrazed land rapidly succumbing to the stranglehold of weeds. It was happening in every field, on every hillside: the pretty, 'natural' landscape with its velvet-soft green contours, so beloved of visiting town-dwellers, was produced by its flocks of sheep and no more natural than a shed of battery chickens. She was reminded of the old gardener's reply to the minister who had congratulated him on what a good job he and the Almighty together had made of the garden: 'Aye, you should have just seen it when the Almighty had it to himsel'!'

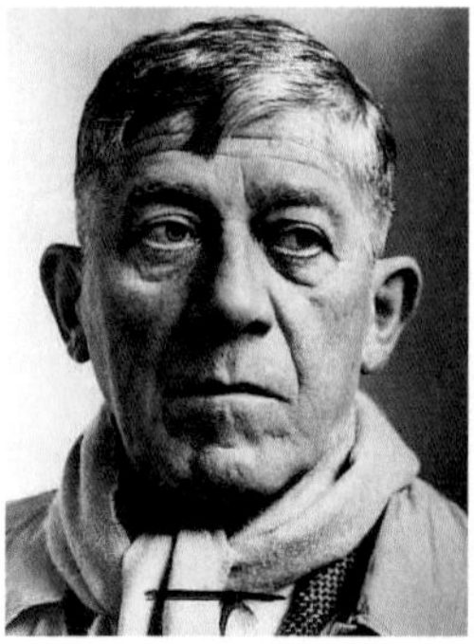

The final 'pair of eyes' from furth of the Shire is that of a painter, no less than one of the giants of European expressionism **Oskar Kokoschka** (1886-1980), whose little-known connection with the county comes as a delightful surprise.

In 1938 Kokoschka took refuge from the Nazis by fleeing to Britain. He lived and worked in London and at Polperro in Cornwall but also had six periods of residence between 1941 and 1946 in the Machars. No artist's hovel for Kokoschka: he was lent the grand House of Elrig, Gavin Maxwell's childhood home (see The Writers). The house had been bought by Kokoschka's friend and patron Professor Emil Korner, a wealthy industrialist and economist who had also secured political asylum in the UK.

Though Kokoschka complained that 'it continually rains here', his Wigtownshire sojourns were welcome escapes from the London blitz, a balm for the depression that he felt in the face of wartime destruction. 'It helps me to forget the awful civilisation and the state of the world we live in at present', he wrote to an acquaintance.

His Elrig sketchbooks are packed with details of the countryside and its wildlife, which he would later incorporate into his bigger works. He and his wife Olda enjoyed observing the characters around Elrig. Olda wrote to a friend: 'We have met some queer neighbours here, hunting and shooting people in eerie overgrown houses without anybody to look after them...I do not see how they all do not die in the winter of rheumatism and lumbago'.

Several major works by Kokoschka have been identified as

Wigtownshire output, though, given their weirdness, it certainly helps to have been told so by the experts. One in particular, entitled *Loreley*, is in the collection of the Tate Galleries in London. It is a busily peopled seascape apparently based on the legend of the Rhine maiden who lured sailors to their deaths. It is supposed to be a satire on British pretensions to maritime supremacy. The artist himself described the picture:

> Britannia no longer rules the waves; inaction has lasted too long; an octopus swims away with a trident, the emblem of marine power. Queen Victoria, who built up the British fleet into a dominant position, rides a shark and stuffs white, brown and black sailors into its mouth. Only the frog on her hand refuses to accept the same fate: it represents Ireland, where there are no reptiles except frogs.

Phew! The water may well be that of Luce Bay and the tall structure on the horizon may well be the Mull of Galloway lighthouse but, frankly, they may equally well be just figments of his agitated imagination. *Loreley*, we are told, had been begun in Wigtownshire as a more straightforward landscape but its theme darkened on his return to war-damaged London, where dejection once again took hold of his vision.

Index